DELIGHT 1918 - 1976

If ever there was an angel in human form it was
Delight. "When she shall die, take her, and form her
into little stars, and she shall make the face of
heaven so fine that all the world will be in love with
night." - Shakespeare

Grieve No More, Beloved:
The Book of Delight

by
Ormond McGill

Crown House Publishing Limited
www.crownhouse.co.uk

Published by
Crown House Publishing Ltd
Crown Buildings
Bancyfelin, Carmarthen, Wales, SA33 5ND, UK
www.crownhouse.co.uk
and
Crown House Publishing Company, LLC
P.O. Box 2223, Williston, VT. 05495
www.crownhousepublishing.com

British Library Catalouging-in-Publications Data
A catalog entry for this book is available
from the British Library.

LCCN: 2003106581

Paper Edition
10 digit ISBN: 1904424163
13 digit ISBN: 9781904424161

Cloth Edition
10 digit ISBN: 1899836004
13 digit ISBN: 9781899836000

Printed in the United States of America

FOREWORD

by Cherith Powell

(Principal of the Atkinson-Ball College of Hypnotherapy and HypnoHealing, and President of the Corporation of Advanced Hypnotherapy).

I have known Ormond McGill for nine years, during which time he has been a source of inspiration to me, both personally and in the field of hypnotherapy. He is known worldwide as "The Dean of American Hypnotists". His knowledge of how the mind works is unsurpassed.

He has written numerous books about hypnosis, but it is my view that this, his latest book, is the most important one of all. It is one that everyone will need at some time in their lives; that is following the death of a loved one.

My own soul-mate, Bill Atkinson-Ball, who was a very close friend of Ormond McGill, died in 1992. Bill had been my teacher, my partner, and my best friend. Our lives were completely intertwined. How I wish that I could have had this book close by me at that time. My own knowledge and research into the after-life helped me considerably during those first few black months, and I was grateful for the knowledge that I had. It helps so much to be able to look at "death" for what it is, i.e. a transition, a moving onwards to a new life.

So many times during the bereavement process one asks oneself "Where are you?". The Book of Delight answers this question in great and beautiful detail, giving reassurance and a complete certainty in survival of "life".

In my own work with bereaved people, I have found that there is always the tendency to "hang on". That is only natural. But the release, the letting go of a loved one does not mean more loss, just the opposite, and often brings an awareness and closeness far beyond that which could be found in the physical life.

It is my privilege to know Ormond McGill, a man of warmth,

sincerity and humility, and it is therefore my pleasure to write the foreword to this book, and hope that it will be an inspiration and source of comfort to you, the reader.

Cherith Powell
Autumn 1994

THE STORY OF DELIGHT

Here and now in your possession is a <u>Wonder Full</u> book. As it is written from a transcendental source it can function as a guidebook of life beyond death.

Each person is an individual consciousness of which there is none other exactly the same in the entire Universe. Each individual life is filled with a multitudinous variety of experiences personal to each one. Such is true on both sides of what is called "The Veil". Yet basic to all is a foundation of similarity and unity, as each is interconnected with the other - thus it is possible to give a pattern of fundamental types of experiences one finds on THE OTHER SIDE. Delight gives you an outline of these fundamental types to form a matrix of knowing of your continuation of existence after death which is the heritage of everyone.

THAT IS WHAT THE BOOK OF DELIGHT IS ALL ABOUT.

As she wrote the book which I have scribed at her dictation from beyond, it is fitting that I should tell you some things about Delight. Delight entered into form this lifetime through the union of Ray and Anna May Olmstead. The date of her birth was April 11, 1918. On seeing the newborn child her mother exclaimed: "This girl will be a delight". She was named Delight right then and there, and no other name could suit her equally.

I met Delight when she was twenty-one in 1939. Four years later, in 1943, we were married in Santa Monica, California. She was 25 and I was 30. We honeymooned in La Jolla, one of the beauty spots on the Californian coast adjacent to San Diego. The very name La Jolla, in Spanish, means "The Jewel".

My marriage to Delight was heaven on earth: a meeting of "twin souls". Peaceful, serene, supportive, an ever spiralling upward of love. Wonderful - until she died in 1976. Then hell crashed in upon me. When you lose someone whom you love and who loves you, it is devastating. To me, it was an experience like being cut in half with a knife. Everything seemed grey: the sky, the flowers, the trees, everything.

THEN A MIRACLE HAPPENED:

Approximately three weeks after her passing onward, about 3:30 each morning, I would awaken and it would seem that I could sense Delight coming in and lying down beside me, and she whispered in my ear a telling of her adventures on THE OTHER SIDE. Yet I thought it must be fantasy, so I turned over and returned to sleep. Upon awakening it would be gone. The visitation was repeated for a week - night after night. I could not sleep anyway, so I decided I might as well get up and write down what her consciousness was telling me. My thought was that possibly it might produce an interesting paper on these mysteries which mankind has speculated upon from time immemorial. To my surprise this went on for three months, telling of the nature of life beyond death, and brought answers to many questions. The result you now hold in your hands: THE BOOK OF DELIGHT.

When this was complete, the visitations from her ended, and I sent the manuscript in to my literary agent in New York for publication consideration. The response came back that it was beautiful but too personal for general publication. It belonged to me alone. I knew that this was true and also I knew that it was not for me alone: it was a gift for everyone on the planet, especially those who suffer the loss of a loved one.

So I depersonalized the manuscript a little here and there, and added some poetic thoughts from other sources that, likewise, pertained to insights about the deathlessness of all mankind - to add titbits of extra understanding.

Thus before you now is this book which is being first published by the Anglo American Book Company Ltd in England and circulated throughout the British Isles, and hence on to circulation throughout the world. My heartfelt appreciation to Martin and Glenys Roberts and also to Cherith Powell of the Atkinson-Ball College of Hypnotherapy & HypnoHealing for making it possible to share with others that which removed grief from my heart and brought joy in knowing that loved ones are never lost.

In closing this personal prologue, what more can I say than that if there was ever an angel in human form it was Delight. And, as Shakespeare so beautifully expressed it:

"When she shall die
Make her into
Little stars,
And all the world
Shall fall in love with night."

Ormond McGill
California, September 1994

TABLE OF CONTENTS

INTRODUCTION

This is a book about death, and yet it is a joyous book. Really it is a cause for celebration, for it tells that loved ones are never lost, about life after death and about your immortality. I wrote the book, and Delight spirited it.

My beloved wife, Delight, died of cancer, as many others have died. She was seated partially upright in her bed, her eyes open just a little, with a serene look upon her face which seemed to be saying: "This is wonderful". I choked up, kissed her stilled lips twice, and they led me from the hospital room.

When a loved one dies, thoughtful relatives and friends will flood your home with flowers and all manner of nice things, and your post is filled with hosts of beautiful sympathy cards expressing in many kind ways: "Bear up - find happiness again, for you still have the wonderful memories of the departed to comfort you. . .". Lovely sentiments, and surely appreciated. But, honestly, how much more one wants than just memories. One wants an assurance that the beloved lives on beyond death, that the separation is but a temporary matter, that in time you will be united again.

The two weeks following her death were a time of tears for me. It was a gulf of loneliness, yet I ate and slept, even if fitfully, as the body demands that. In the middle of the third week I awoke in the early hours of the morning with a strong sense of Delight's presence near me. The experience in every way was of her consciousness that I had known so intimately for the 33 years of our life together. Her presence, as it came to me, was in the nature of a subjective experiencing of an objective phenomenon that was immediately recognizable as her individual self. I will explain a little . . . every person radiates a certain personal magnetism that is distinctly of themselves. When you hold your loved one in your arms, you are certain to feel it. This "flow of feeling" is as individual a mark of a specific personality as is one's thumbprint. Between Delight and myself the "flow of feeling" was remarkable, and even at the lowest ebb of her illness never ceased to be of high intensity, and identified her spirit (as distinct from her disease-racked body) on the instant.

To me, the forces of love and personal magnetism are things of the soul, and remain unaffected even with the body's decline and eventual passing. Lovers experience this intimate exchange continuously. As Delight's body declined in physical health, the strength of her spirit increased in direct ratio. I could see it in her eyes. I could feel it in her body. It was ever-present and still is. Far more than just memory, it is a thing alive and immortal. It is a testimonial to the existence and the continuance of life after death and beyond.

The personal nearness of Delight following her death brought many insights which would flood my being,[1] insights which spoke of death and what lies beyond death. It was a communication between our spirits, as it were, which was as intense as any I had ever felt during our many years of superlatively happy life on earth together. As the days passed, the clarity of this communication (really communion expresses it more accurately than does communication) increased so that we could deal with specifics of what lies beyond the grave or a mound of ashes sealed within a jar. It was a love experience.

I questioned this very matter of spirit communications and on this Delight counselled that when a loved one dies there is a natural desire to communicate with the departed. There is only one type of spirit communication which has real value both to the disembodied soul and those still embodied, and that is a "spiritual rapport". Such communication seeks no phenomena of manifestation, but is a continuation of personal intimacy between souls, both in-body and out-of-body and/or within form or without form on both sides of death. It is a communion maintained as a sympathetic connection with those near and dear by ties of love or friendship in both realms, and has a highly spiritual nature entirely devoid of nearness in terms of physical space.

The ties and bonds between the disembodied soul and the soul still in the flesh in earth-life may be thought of as spiritual filaments, something like a transcendent form of telepathic rapport. When the disembodied soul is thinking of the loved one on earth, the latter

---

[1] I use the term **"flood my being"** as this is the manner in which insights from Delight occur. They come in as a whole, as a totality. One moment they are not there, the next they are there. Embellishing her insights and putting them into orderly form so that they may be shared with others is my position as writer of this book.

frequently experiences feelings akin to the physical nearness of the departed person. In the same way the disembodied soul experiences a sense of nearness from the person in the flesh when the latter is thinking of the former. Both become a channel unto the other, and both benefit from the close communion.

Such experiences come as a wonderful proof of the continuation of life after death. The communication can be as great in degree as if they were alive and here. Feelings of love and affection between separated souls is wondrous, for both seem to be comforted and strengthened and even to find pleasure and joy. It is a beautiful phenomenon. It may be regarded as a sacred relationship. Let this "love bond" be the means of spiritual communication as a rewarding experience.

Thus, from Delight many insights telling about death and deathlessness have come through to me. They have brought great solace and understanding and, while many of these experiences are personal, the truth of what they represent and the truths of what they tell - from the position of transcendental wisdom - are most assuredly not exclusive. They belong to everyone and provide a comfort I happily share with all who hold in their hearts a beloved one who has passed onwards, even as Delight.

There is so much that one wishes to know about death and life beyond death, so many questions to be asked and so many answers to be sought, that the search is wondrous. Delight tells it so beautifully and with such depth of enlightenment. Here is assurance that loved ones live on after death, that any heartfelt separation is temporary, and that those who love will be united again. Furthermore this book will remove your own fear of dying, for it affords a glimpse of what lies behind the "Veil of Death". It assures you of your own immortality.

I will ask the questions and Delight will light these pages with her answers.

CHAPTER 1

THE PATHWAY OF CONSCIOUSNESS

From an awareness of Delight's consciousness come these insights about deathlessness which are frequently beyond normal knowing, and, since they are hers, I phrase - when it is appropriate - her insights within quotation marks:

"If I am to answer your questions about death and what lies beyond death, in order that you will understand fully, we must relate together with a high form of awareness (consciousness). For while I use words in the telling of these matters, actually the words are only used to take you to that which is beyond words to describe, that which is transcendental. Your understanding must come from your own inner awareness of these truths, as only then may you come to learn about that which is eternal and immortal.

"If the Universe were entirely based upon exact laws of cause and effect, it would be easier to tell you these facts, but such is not the case. There is in the Universe that which is unpredictable, a sentience. A vast consciousness seems to pervade the entirety of Existence. One senses it while in form in the physical world, and one senses it equally while in the formless in the non-physical world.

"To the very peak of consciousness we apply the term 'God'. The greater one advances in consciousness, the more God-like one becomes. Consciousness is immortal and death cannot touch it at all, but death can provide a means for more awareness, and awareness is another name for consciousness.

"While living in the human body, Man can know four types of consciousness. It is well that you learn these for the betterment of your understanding of death.

"Let's refer to the lowest form of consciousness as **unconscious consciousness**. This is the state of consciousness which is absolutely 'asleep' - the state of matter. By way of an example, a rock exists in such a state of consciousness. 'Unconscious consciousness' is pre-life. In this state there is no freedom because freedom enters through consciousness. In this state, there is only cause and effect. The 'Law of Cause and Effect' is absolute in relation to matter; freedom is unknown. Freedom enters only as a shadow of consciousness. The more conscious you become, the more free.

"Physical science is much confined to the realm of cause and effect, as it deals mostly with matter. However even here the nuclear physicist is beginning to enter into a world which is beyond cause and effect, and the principle of uncertainty is beginning to arise. The principle of uncertainty means the principle of freedom. Now scientists are beginning to recognize that the deeper they penetrate into matter, and the more it appears to develop aspects of consciousness, there comes a certain quality of freedom. As yet in its evolution of consciousness, a rock is in a state below mind. Obviously, there is no 'self' in the rock because, without the mind, self cannot exist.

"Let's refer to the next form of consciousness, in ascending order of awareness, as **simple consciousness**. This is the state of life pre-self-consciousness. The first realm was matter. Now comes this form . . . trees, animals, etc. The rock cannot move. The rock has no life visible anywhere. The trees have more life, and animals still more. The tree is rooted in the ground and cannot move much. A little freedom certainly is there, but the animal has more freedom. It can move. This is the realm of simple consciousness. It is rudimentary consciousness coming into being. The rock is absolutely unconscious, but you cannot say that a tree is unconscious in the same sense. It is unconscious of self, but something of the beginning of consciousness is filtering in.

"Animals have more of this consciousness. The animal has a little bit of freedom. It can choose a few things: it can be temperamental; it can be in a good mood and be friendly towards you; it can be in a bad mood and be unfriendly towards you. A little bit of decision has come into its being - just the beginning. The self is not yet integrated . . . it is a very loose self, but it is coming up. The structure is taking shape, the form is arising.

"The animal is past-oriented. It lives mostly in relation to the past.

The animal has scant idea of the future. It does not plan for the future. Very little does it think ahead. Once in a while it will think ahead, but only in a sketchy manner, possibly a few hours to when feeding time will be. But the animal cannot think about one month or two months in the future. The animal cannot conceive of years; it has no calendar, no time concept. It is mostly past-oriented. Whatever has happened in the past it expects to happen in the future too, as the past dominates it. Thus in animals it will be seen that time is entering through the past; self is entering through the past.

"The next form of consciousness - the third form - is that of **self-consciousness**. This is the state of awareness in which that which we call 'mind' enters, and self-consciousness arises. Consciousness is advancing, and along with it enters the self. Self-consciousness comes, bringing in the idea of 'I'. Reflection starts, thinking starts, personality comes into being. And with the mind comes future orientation; man lives in the future - animals live in the past. With the coming of self-consciousness and living in the future is a higher consciousness.

"In this state Man advances his freedom over the limited freedom which animals have, as the freedom of choice has entered. That means he can choose. He can go to visit this place or that place. He can do this or that kind of work. He can go to the church of his choice. More freedom of will has entered, and freedom of will is one of man's greatest gifts.

"I will now tell you about transcendental consciousness, which is also termed **cosmic consciousness**. This is the fourth state of consciousness and is the highest form of awareness of which man is capable while still living in the body. It is the state of consciousness which all the great Masters have experienced; Christ, Buddha, Lao Tzu - all who have been known among men as the 'Enlightened Ones' - who have tried to explain to Man the transcendental and tell him of his immortality. In this state you have total freedom. In it one's mind becomes linked with the Totality, with Existence. It is well-termed 'cosmic consciousness', for it is linked with the Cosmos. This is a form of consciousness in which real freedom is experienced for it is beyond choice. Real freedom happens only when one's life becomes so total in each moment that there is no need to decide. There is no need to make choices, for Existence itself decides.

"**In this state of consciousness one moves beyond knowledge to 'knowing'.** That is what intuition means. That is the light with which I flood your Being in telling of these truths. Intellect lives in tuition. Others have taught you. Via intuition nobody has to teach you; it comes from within. It grows out of you. It is a flowering of your Being. It is from the transcendental. This is the quality of consciousness called Cosmic Consciousness. Some Masters have called it 'the Omega Point'. Buddha called it 'Nirvana'. Jainas called it 'Moksha'. Christ called it 'God the Father'. These are different names for the same thing.

"Choicelessness is real freedom. You don't choose; you simply become totally aware. Insight starts functioning. Intuition starts functioning. It is towards this highest form of consciousness that I wish you to advance, as it is then that I can best bring to you an understanding of death and beyond. For in these realms you must move beyond beliefs and even beyond that upon which mind can reason, as in the transcendental there is not much that can be expressed in solid black and white. The beautiful hues of the colours of knowing what lies between must be appreciated.

"How can you recognize the 'knowing' which comes via transcendental consciousness? You cannot recognize it with your mind. You can recognize it only by a resonating within your being. It is like an electric spark that suddenly shoots up your spine. It is like a singing. Judge the truth of what I tell you by that which sings deep within yourself.

"Consciousness is of great importance, for in consciousness is found the real you which is beyond death, and thus through death can be found not one's termination of being, but rather an expansion of being. Possibly putting it in this manner will be helpful to your understanding . . .

"Consider Existence in relation to consciousness and review: a stone exists and is not considered alive; a tree exists and is considered alive but its consciousness is rudimentary; an animal is considered alive with recognizable consciousness; a man exists and is considered alive inclusive of a developed awareness of self-consciousness, with a potential of evolving upwards to an awareness of universal reality. What is awareness of universal reality but cosmic consciousness? And what is cosmic consciousness but God-consciousness? And to know God is to recognize immortality. What is immortality but life beyond death? What is life beyond death but the transition of life to more abundant life?

"Yet further expansion on the matter of consciousness provides an understanding in which the illusory nature of death is revealed. Consciousness may be regarded as a yardstick of awareness and, like all that exists in nature whatever its realm, and whatever its roots, it is a matter of energy, a matter of vibration. As all things exist in accordance with the manner of its vibration, consciousness (in one of its diverse forms) is to be found in each thing with its awareness level differing markedly. Consciousness may be considered a spiral - starting low, proceeding upwards in a graduating scale, to culminate in the consciousness of God. It may also be looked at in this way: God has enough consciousness to be God - an omnipotent universal consciousness of which each person is a part. That is, each is conscious to the degree that it is, but the potential is there for a steady advancement of consciousness to infinite consciousness (God-Consciousness).

"As a formula it may be stated that the lower the vibrational rate of a state of consciousness, the less its awareness. Death, in freeing man from his physical body, increases his vibrational rate[2] and, in direct ratio, expands his consciousness which makes him more alive, and to be more alive removes the termination sentiments of death, and death is seen for what it actually is, a transition to a state of being even more alive. This shatters the mystery of life beyond death.

"Thus, know the truth that the God Consciousness pervades and is in all that is of the Universe, Existence itself, the Isness. As we are part

---

[2]The term "vibrational rate" may be taken literally or in a symbolic sense. The choice is yours.

of that Universe and Universal Consciousness, so are we part of God, and His Consciousness pervades our Being. Why do we pray to God as though He were in some distant place and ask that He grant us favours at His whim, when in reality God Consciousness is every bit as much within us as it is without?

"Truly we are created in the image of God and His power is our power. It is not some special favour. It is our birthright. It is our Isness. The secret of our true purpose of being lies in raising our consciousness level to harmonize with God Consciousness. This is what is meant by obtaining 'Oneness with God'. Such is the true purpose of Existence for every soul - to evolve thus upwards - and life after life is seen as stepping stones along the pathway - as we advance onward in expanding consciousness to find ultimately this 'Oneness with God'. It is then that we realize our Divinity, and appreciate that our demise at death is an absolute impossibility.

"There is so much to tell you. Flood your being with the asking and I will flood your being with the knowing."

CHAPTER 2

THE GREATEST LIE IN THE WORLD

As I sought direct answers to the matter of death, I flooded my being with questions and sought insights from the consciousness of Delight. Responding to my questions, she flooded my being with this:

"You are asking about that which really is not, for the reality is that the concept of death is the greatest lie with which man has deceived himself throughout the ages. In believing this lie, Man has created his greatest fear - for the fear of death forms the root of all his fears. The truth is that everything is eternal and immortal; that nothing dies, that nothing can die. There is only one thing that is a lie, and that is death. Only death is impossible, and everything else is possible.

"That is why I propose that you expand your consciousness, for then you will understand what I tell you in this my book. For if you become aware, you become aware of the deathless within you. If you are only self-conscious, you are living in the mortal body only, then how greatly you will fear death but if you can move beyond that to recognize yourself as a consciousness within the body and not of the body, then you are touching the truth and are moving beyond the lie of death.

"If you can understand this deeply enough, it will remove your fear of death, but it is not easy, for the fear of death is a very basic fear, for death cannot be destroyed! You can reject it with your mind, but you cannot deny it for it is always there causing a trembling throughout your whole life.

"In the West people are very scared because they fight continuously against death. To make it personal, you love life; you respect life. That is why old people are not more respected and young people are - the world is considered a young man's world. Old people are not much respected because they have moved further towards death than you. They are already in its grip. Youth is respected in the West, yet the truth is that youth is a transitory phenomenon. It is already passing from your hands.

"In the East old people are respected, because in the East death is more generally respected. Life is looked upon as just a part and death the culmination of life. Life is just the process and death is the crescendo of the process. Life is just the moving, while death is the reaching. And both are one!

"If you can feel the poetry of this in your Being it will help you. Death is the flowering of life . . . death is the flower. Life is the tree and the tree is there for the flower. The flower is not there for the tree. The tree should be happy, and the tree should dance when the flower comes. If you can feel this, then death will be accepted without fear, not only accepted without fear, but will be welcomed as a Divine guest. When it knocks at the door, it means the Universe is ready to receive you back.

"Kahlil Gibran expresses this beautifully in this little quotation about death from his writing: 'Only when you drink from the river of silence shall you indeed sing. And when you have reached the mountain top, then shall you begin to climb. And when the earth shall claim your limbs, then shall you truly dance.'

"All men, in the East or the West, will feel an instinctive respect for death if they pause to feel it, and they do pause instinctively (even if only for a few moments) before one who is dead, for a man in death is to be respected; he is ahead of you. This respect is as it should be, for death is a door through which a man has passed. You cannot see him beyond that 'door' any more than you can see a person in the next room when the door is closed.

"Understand this; death is a door. It is not a stopping. Awareness (consciousness) moves, but your body remains at the door. The body is left outside the temple, but your Awareness enters the temple. It is the most subtle phenomenon. Life is nothing before it.

"Appreciate that basically life is a preparation for dying, and truly only those are wise who learn during life how to die, for in this 'knowing' you come to understand the deepest meaning of life. Life is a preparation. It is a training. For life is not the end - it is just a discipline to learn the art of dying. If at the thought of death you start feeling fear, it means that you have not yet known life because life never dies.

"Life cannot die. If at the thought of death you start trembling it means that somewhere you have become identified with the body only, with the mechanism. The mechanism is to die. The mechanism cannot be eternal because the mechanism depends on many things - it is a conditioned phenomenon. Awareness (consciousness) is unconditional. It does not depend on anything. And this awareness is YOU.

"All during your lifetime in the physical world you are repeatedly told the importance of learning the 'art of living'. This is fine and as it should be, but it is equally important that you learn the 'art of dying'. Understand this . . . to live life fully you must learn the 'art of living'. To live death fully (which means to live fully in the otherside of life which is beyond death) you must learn the 'art of dying'. To die means to be forced to give up all control of your material body, its organs and its senses - to relinquish this control when, for physical reasons, the organism is no longer able to sustain its life. Death is ever coming and it can happen at any time. The very essence of the 'art of dying' consists of being ready at any moment of your earthly life - in the midst of the fullness of living - to be willing to make the transition via the phenomenon of death from this life to the next phase of life and to do this willingly, joyfully and with confident serenity. The art is to attain this inner attitude, which first must come from an understanding of what death is all about; the fact that the body is a temporary housing which is occupied by SELF (soul, being, individual consciousness - call it what you will), which is immortal and exists eternally.

"The reason that you grieve over the loss of a loved one is that death seems so final. It seems so much to cut off everything, to shatter tomorrows together, but, in knowing the truth of immortality, this is obviously an illusion, and there is no termination at all. Life goes on in a new dimension following death. It seems so distant because in-body you live in one dimension (of the form) while out-of-body the beloved who has passed through the transition of death lives in another (of the formless). But love can cross this gap even this very moment.

"If you have loved somebody and you didn't miss an opportunity to show that love, then even when death comes there is no need for mourning. If you really love, death cannot take anything from you. Indeed death may even become an opportunity, an opening of a new door.

"You loved the friend when he was visible, when he was in body, and you loved him so deeply that you started feeling, through your love, the invisibleness of him. Then death takes the body. Now love can flow totally. You were already discovering the spiritual dimension of your beloved lover/friend and now death has removed the last obstacle. Now you can see with absolute clarity. Death has given you an opportunity to see whether you really loved or not, because if love's eyes cannot penetrate so that you can see that which is not body, that which is beyond matter, that which is invisible, then it is not love. You will be weeping and mourning and you will be thinking that you are crying for the friend who has gone, but it is not so. You are weeping for yourself.

"If you really love and feel the immortality of the one who has passed out of form into the formless, then there is no need for grieving. Grieve if you like, but there is no need for it. It is impossible not to feel sadness when a friend departs, but sadness and mourning are two entirely different things. Sadness has a beauty of its own, a depth, a silence that always comes when one encounters death. That sadness will reveal something within you that life before did not reveal, and you will know not only the immortality of the one who has departed first, but your own as well. Your own trembling stops. Death is very deep, like sadness, but sadness is not mourning, sadness has its own delight. Now you will know that the beloved is not dead at all and that there is no death for you as well for your love has bridged the gap of the truth of immortality. That life goes on. That love goes on.

"To help you understand the true nature of death, I will sum up these matters: **all physical life is transitory and temporary, and be not dismayed by this fact. Rather consider your current life and the next life as one life. How then can you lose loved ones? A bit of patience. A little waiting. That is all.**

"This is sufficient for me to say about the lie of death. Let me now light your path to a knowing of what dying is all about."

CHAPTER 3

WHAT IS IT TO DIE?

Insights about death and life after death came into my consciousness in repeated sessions from Delight. She continued to tell what dying is in relation to how it will be experienced:

"The only absolute certainty you have in life is that you are going to die. The moment you are born you start dying. Every breath you take brings you closer to death. It can be said that a man's lifespan may be measured by how many breaths he will take during that lifespan. To go deeper, all is relative since it may also be said that a breath is to a man's single lifespan as one lifespan is to the time that life has been on the earth.

"First it must be understood that life and death are each part of the other. Each is simply a differing phase of the continuum of the individual. To 'die' is merely the passing forward from a completed episode of Existence. The truth is that there is no death at all - there is only life - but it is difficult to understand when it is expressed that way because only positives and negatives can be readily understood in relation to our Existence. Therefore let us say that life is the fact and death is the non-fact, so the mind may better understand, unless you already have sufficient awareness to drop duality and appreciate the Oneness in all that is.

"So I will express life and death in a positive and negative sense and tell of phenomena which will occur to each individual as a consciousness experience in dying, which is the 'Veil' that shrouds the space which is without space . . . the Shadowland lying between life and death. 'Shadowland' is a sort of symbolic description but actually it is as real as any space on earth. It is mysterious in its own way but really it is quite wonderful.

"This 'Shadowland' is the lower plane of Existence which awaits just beyond the doorway of death. It is a space beyond space designed for your (I could use the term 'your soul's') cleansing prior to its advancing to higher states of Being in the life beyond death - or its prompt returning for another bout with physical Existence. Two sides of Existence for everyone is the truth. Really just calling them the positive and negative aspects of the same thing comes closest to the truth. We can also express it as the world in which you find yourself after making the transition of death from the familiar physical world.

"Beyond this Shadowland lies the world of spirit. I like to call this the 'mind-world', as to me that explains it best - it is so spiritual in nature, or I can just call it the two sides of Existence, both worlds to be lived in (I should say 'experienced' for accuracy), and so inter-related as to present difficulty in distinguishing one from the other. Indeed even to your consciousness it may be difficult to distinguish between the two, for what the mind has recognized as 'thought patterns of personal Existence' in physical life can be repeated closely in mental (astral) life.

"Nature is efficient, and since you have had many life experiences, do not expect a new mould to be suddenly cast about you in the next phase beyond death. Really as far as your consciousness goes, perception on one side will seem much the same as on the other, except in appreciating a greater sense of freedom of Being in the mind-world over the physical embodiment left behind for a time. There is mind linked with spirit ever present both in the physical world and in the realm of its greater freedom, **for to die is but to free your SELF** (self is the correct term as it is inclusive of mind/spirit) **from its encasement in body**, with its limitation of manifesting in three dimensional space.

"Do not however build any illusions that the passing over to the other side is going to make you completely new or solve all the great mysteries for you or explain the true meaning of God. For it is not so. True you will know more than you do on the physical side, as much of the 'forgetfulness' will be lifted from your mind. The totalities of your experiences of past lives will spread before you but you will still be yourself and will advance in direct ratio to the status of your thoughts. Remember your thinking has determined your present status, and your present thinking will determine your future status, for 'as a man thinketh in his heart so is he'.

"The doorway of death provides a wonderful opportunity to achieve your fondest wishes. If your wish is Emancipation, the opportunity is there. If your wish is a heavenly state, the opportunity is there. If your wish is more of the same status in the physical world, that it may continue, the opportunity is there. Or if you wish a new status in Existence, the opportunity is there. **And it is a real choice, only dependent upon your own awareness as to the choice you can make.**

"The truth is that nobody is producing nature and nobody is stopping nature. Existence is taking care of itself, and all Man has to do is accept it as it is. This is a beautiful understanding for it removes the yoke of karma and the yoke of sin and all such worries from humanity, so really there is no problem at all. Things are just as they are, so there is nothing for you to do. You can just watch Existence happening and enjoy it. You can be there with Existence and in that 'being there' is freedom. For perfection of your Being you have to recognize and become aware of that fact. It is thus that a man becomes holy. In accepting nature, in living naturally moment-to-moment there is holiness because you are WHOLE, not because you have become a saint. All you have to do is awaken and realize your own SELFHOOD to recognize its perfection of Being.

"It may be that at this moment your consciousness is not advanced enough to appreciate this truth I am telling you, but in time you will. Your consciousness is of your own making (entirely in relation to its degree of awareness) and it is unlikely that these insights will change it. However at least let this understanding remove from you worries about fixed laws of punishments of karma or sin, lordly judgments or heaven/hell concepts after you die - for the truth is, there are none except those you create for yourself.

"Further, appreciate this truth if you can - your SELF (call it your SOUL or whatever you please) is immortal and perfect, and recognition of that perfection will inevitably come to every soul. That is what is meant by 'Enlightenment'; recognizing this truth that there is nobody to damn your soul or to praise your soul. It is just as it is.

"**Your status in relation to Existence is entirely to the degree of your awakening to this truth**. Every Master, like Christ, has been trying to tell mankind of this - that the birthright of entering the 'Kingdom of

God' is there just for the taking - but most take so long to recognize their heritage, going through life after life until the awakening eventually dawns.

"There is however no hurry unless it is your wish that there be a hurry, so let your desires be what your desires are, but free them of bondages that cause you concern and accept death as a gift. Be not unwilling to die when it is time to die. If you can enter death consciously you will find it a most rewarding experience. However if you die in your sleep (unconscious), there is no need to fear for your subconscious knows well the process; it has been through the transition many times. Fight not the entrance into death when it is time. Let yourself flow and enter it gently and you will be helped.

"Be not detained when the time of death is at hand by the hopeless pleadings of those remaining who entreat you not to leave them and fill your mind with thoughts of how urgently you are still needed in the physical world. Be not deterred by such thoughts, for there is no reason to suppose needfulness and usefulness are the exclusive properties of the physical side. Most assuredly needfulness and usefulness, in countless ways, are to be performed in the realm of your Existence which lies beyond death.

"Lest some of this seem a little 'deep' to your awareness at this time, appreciate that it will all become perfectly clear when you reach a transcendental level, for it is then that you can **become a witness to dying**. Then you will spontaneously understand. It is well that we go into this matter a bit about becoming a 'witness to dying', as it will change your attitude towards death - this is important."

CHAPTER 4

BECOMING A WITNESS TO DYING

The insights from Delight's consciousness to my consciousness continued, and I have recorded such accordingly:

"As long as you fear death, Existence will be your enemy, for the reality is that inevitably Existence will lead you down that path. You will note that I capitalize 'Existence' in this text, the same as I would capitalize 'God'. Is there any difference as it is presented here? For the truth is you are not going to die in the sense of non-being any more than that Existence is going to die and become non-being.

"Existence continues eternally, and as you are a part of Existence so will you. Understand this and you will understand that Existence is your friend - it is yours to enjoy. Even the dying experience is to be enjoyed. When you can appreciate this truth you are ready to take a plunge into learning the facts about the personal experience of dying, and of what awaits you beyond death. The best way to experience this is by becoming a **witness** to life . . . and death.

"There is an ancient oriental teaching called Tantra which has as its symbol the wheel. The rim of the wheel represents the hurly-burly world which revolves about you constantly. If a person is caught up in life on the rim of the wheel then there is no real peace but a wheel has a hub at its centre which is the quiet point. Man is like the wheel, outside (as body) he lives on the rim but deep inside he has a quiet centre in which his real SELF (Soul) dwells. When he recognizes this, and wishes to withdraw from the activity on the rim of the wheel, from his 'Centre of Being' he can just watch and **witness** and learn of truth . . . of the truth of his true status in Existence, of the reality of what life is all about and of his deathlessness.

"All the great Masters have looked at life in this manner, for to become a **witness** is to take a position in higher consciousness. Then instead of moving in the horizontal one moves in the vertical. Instead of having points of view about the world, one has points to view. That is what is meant by becoming a **witness**, and it applies not only to life in the physical world, but through the experience of dying as well and on into the beyond. If you can take all your experiences as a **witness** (with your SELF as an observer of the happenings of death), all the confusion which death produces for many can become a fascinating experience for you.

"There is a Tantric technique of meditation which shows the way to obtain this high level of consciousness of witnessing, and through using this process the difference in your viewing of both life and death becomes tremendous. This technique is expressed in this sutra:

> 'This so-called universe appears
> as a juggling, a picture show.
> To be happy, look upon it so.'

"To put into practice this technique, simply change your point of view. Come to look upon this whole world (and the next world as well following death) as the reverse side of the coin. You will be equally conscious in both. Come to look upon all that happens to you in the drama of Existence as a stage play that you are witnessing. And in this witnessing, for the first time, you begin to appreciate what Existence is all about.

"If you can come to look upon the whole world thus as a drama, with yourself as a witness to the drama rather than caught up in the drama, then you achieve Awareness. All concerns, worries, miseries, whatever, become recognized for their illusory nature. You begin to realize that they exist only because you have been taking life (and death) so seriously. The truth is that Existence is not meant to be an anguish for man. It is meant to be a joy. That is what is expressed in the above sutra: '. . . To be happy, look upon it so'.

"Go to a cinema and watch the spectators who are caught up in the film - some weeping, others laughing and some sexually excited. You may wonder why just a screen can excite viewers to this extent. It is not just a picture to them, not just a story. To them it is real and this is happening all over the world (and in death as well - not only in the cinema). If you can retain that reaction to those cinemagoers and apply this to life, you will never again take life too seriously.

"Come to look at life in this way through this meditation: Look backwards, look forwards, look in every way at what you are, where you are, what your life is all about. It will suddenly appear like a long dream, and everything that you take so seriously this moment becomes inconsequential in the next. It is then that the basic truth of Existence will suddenly dawn upon you, that the whole of your Existence is really just like the playing of a game. The playing of a game has no special purpose. **It is the enjoyment of the playing that is the purpose**. Move this in your consciousness over into the realm of life now and you will see that life has no special goals for you to achieve. It has no special purpose. Rather, it is a celebration! The serious person wants to reach a goal and will even make dying a goal. Then death becomes a very serious thing and its wonderfulness is missed.

"Truly, the way to experience death is to have the time of your life."

CHAPTER 5

WHO ARE YOU?

Delight flooded my Being with these insights about the ego:

"It is important that you know about the ego, for it is important that you know about your SELF as being independent of your physical body if you would fully understand your immortality. Ego is the only thing about yourself which is not real. You are not born with an ego. When you die you recognize that it is not real, yet it can develop in the physical world and seem to become so important as to be all of you. It can become such a covering of your real SELF that you can forget who you are. How anything so transient could take on such a major role is a marvel, yet it does for many people.

"As long as you hold on to ego, you will fear death, for ego identifies itself closely with the body and the body inevitably is going to die. It is the ego of a man which echoes such sentiments as: 'Live fully today, for tomorrow you may die . . . You only go this way once and when it's over, it's over . . . Make yourself important in the world and take from the world all it can give you; claim it now for, if you don't, you will never be able to claim all the good things you deserve to have'.

"Poor suffering man with a great ego! How much he fears death. Beneath the bravado he is really trembling; this is the suffering that comes with wrong thinking, identifying with the ego and missing his true identity. It is only when you recognize the latter that you can understand what Kahlil Gibran expressed poetically, that: 'Life and death are one, even as the river and the sea are one'.

"This matter of ego is so important that it is well that I should emphasize again the truth that Man must drop his ego to discover himself. Many fear to do it as they fear that if their ego is lost, they are lost. This is not the case at all - just understand this - **your individuality and your ego are not the same**. Your individuality is your very personal and special consciousness which is your real identity. Your ego is your false identity - it is the 'I' which the world gives you. Buddha says: 'Ego comes into a person through seven doorways'. Learn of these and you can use them to drop the ego. It is then that you really learn who you are.

"The first doorway by which ego enters is the body self. We are born with a sense of self and feel that there is something which is especially 'me'. Even the way the body functions is especially 'me'. One may express it: 'I am doing this or that' or as 'I am breathing'. The reality is that there is no special 'you' breathing; breathing is just happening.

"The second doorway by which ego enters is self-identity. The child learns its name and realizes that the reflection in the mirror today is the same person it saw in the mirror yesterday. The child recognizes that everything around it is changing, but that image remains the same, so ego has this door to enter by.

"The third doorway by which ego enters is self-esteem. This is concerned with the child's feeling of pride as a result of learning to do a thing on its own and he learns to enjoy doing things because it gives a third door to his ego. The doing of things brings ego in.

"The fourth doorway is self-possession. The child speaks of MY house, MY father, MY mother, MY school - 'Mine' becomes his key word. If you take his toy, he is not so much interested in the toy as he is in feeling 'the toy is MINE, so you cannot take it'. 'Mine' gives a sense of 'me' and 'me' creates 'I' and 'I' creates the ego.

"The fifth doorway is self-image. This refers to how the child sees himself. Through interaction with parents, his teachers, etc. - through praise and punishments - he learns to create a certain image of himself and he is always conscious of how others react to that self-image.

"The sixth doorway is Self as reason. The child learns the way of reason, logic and argument. He learns that he can solve problems. Reason becomes a great support to his self-created Self; to his ego.

"The seventh doorway is striving, having goals, ambitions and desires to become this or that. Future concerns, dreams and long-range objectives appear in this last stage of the ego. It is then that he starts thinking what mark will he make upon the world; what will his greatness be?

"Having explained what the seven doorways to ego are, Buddha then says to back out through them, and then you can lose your ego. Jesus also sums it all up very simply by saying: 'The truth will set you free!' Free from what? Free from your ego, free from the fear that you are going to die. The truth is that there is nothing to really die except that particular ego as it is identified with that particular body.

"Jesus says: 'Leave the things of the world and follow me if you would find your Father in Heaven'. In this he is telling you to leave the things of the world which ego has created as important. Leave all your illusions and false identifications of yourself and recognize yourself even as I recognize myself. It is then that you will find your Divinity and will know your deathlessness. You will know who you are. You will come to know yourself, even as Jesus knew himself, as a 'Son of God', which is like saying that you are as one with the Totality of Existence. It is profound and it is beautiful.

"When Jesus speaks of dropping the ego he is not speaking of modesty. Jesus is only concerned with truth and your recognizing your true identification, not a false one. Jesus named himself the 'Son of God' which would scarcely be called being modest. You can be as proud and immodest as you wish in recognizing your Divinity, for in that pride you are expressing truth.

"The important thing in relation to the matter of death and dying is to recognize your real identity and not your false identity, for in so doing you move beyond the lie of death."

Thus this session with Delight's consciousness ended.

CHAPTER 6

THE EXPERIENCE OF DYING

The next time I felt the consciousness of Delight near me, I asked the question: "What is it like to die?" She answered:

"You now know enough about the nature of death so you can understand. Particularly now that you recognize SELF as something which exists independently of the body (somehow she invariably maintained a sense of continuity to what she was relating) I can tell you what is experienced when you die. Really it is a very personal experience, even an individual one, as it seems different to different persons dependent upon their awareness. I can tell you of my own experiencing.

"First understand that when you die it is a painless process. Whatever pain there is in relation to dying is felt in the body prior to death occurring. Really death comes as a relief. Once the body dies - so that it will no longer maintain (I could say contain) the SELF - the Being begins to release its enmeshment from the no longer functioning body. In leaving the body sensations can be experienced but they are in no sense painful. Indeed most souls leave the dead body with no awareness of the process whatsoever, as it is accomplished in an unconscious sleep-like condition. However it is possible to make the transition from in-body to out-of-body consciously. If you can, by all means do so, as it brings instant awareness of the truth of yourself as an entity existing entirely independent of the body, or even having any need to exist in a body. It is swift 'enlightenment', and that is very good. It is interesting to note that death does not even interrupt the stream of one's consciousness. It can even come (in some cases) as a surprise to find that you are 'dead', as you don't feel any different as far as your consciousness is concerned.

"When the body dies it will seem that irresistible forces are taking hold of you, and you can feel surges of energy passing through the body converging into your Being. Then there comes a sort of pressure that makes you feel as if you are somehow being squeezed out of the body. The closest analogy I can give is that it is much like the squeezing of seeds out of a ripened fruit. As this happens a rush of sound seems to be heard and you have a feeling that you are being drawn through a tunnel. The squeezing sensation continues . . . and you find yourself out-of-body. When this happens you will be amazed at how free you feel. It is rather strange too for in glancing around you can see the room in which you have died, and lying before you is the still form of the old body you have inhabited for so long. In some way it gives you a little pang of nostalgia, as though you are saying 'goodbye' to an old friend whom you know you are not going to see ever again. However any such pangs will soon subside, for in looking down at yourself you will note that you still (to yourself) seem to be the possessor of a body not much different from that which you have left, even though it is of a more tenuous nature.

"If there are others in the room in which you have died you will see them there standing about your dead form. It is both an amusing and a dramatic experience to note these happenings. If you try to communicate with those you see still wearing their physical forms, you find that while you can see them they cannot see you. Indeed the body you now possess is of such a tenuous nature that you can literally pass right through physical matter without obstruction. It seems strange that you cannot make your presence known although some of those of a sensitive nature may seem to be slightly aware (sense) that you are near.

"You will soon be distracted from this viewing of your remains in the physical world as you will note others possessing bodies of the same nature as your new one coming to meet you. Among them you will recognize loved ones who have previously died. It is a loving reunion. You will find that you can communicate easily with these people who are wearing the same kind of body as you now occupy. Among these very personal friends and loved ones one will especially stand out, one whom you will recognize as your 'guide', and it will not be long before you are in deep rapport with this warm spirit Being who assists you in evaluating the life you have just lived. It is a reverie.

"Soon you will sense an exhilarating freedom in your new form, and many who came to see you enter the new phase of life will depart. You will be left alone with your 'guide' who will take you up to what looks like a grey mist before you. Strangely you recognize it since you have been through it before. You know it instinctively as the 'Veil' which divides the physical world from the world of spirit which you are now to enter, and, as your 'guide' beckons, you pass through this into the 'Shadowland' just on the other side of death; this occurs prior to going yet further on into what men at all times have called the 'other side'. I will tell you more of this subsequently.

"This was my conscious experience of dying. Whatever the process is, or whatever the mechanism may be, it is obvious that all the necessary processes are performed instinctively, which is another way of saying that they are performed subconsciously. When we are next close in consciousness I will provide you with more details of these experiences so that you will know more or less what to expect when such experiences become your own. As to the discarded physical body you have left behind - forget it! Once having passed through the 'Veil', it will be of no more interest to you than an old suit of clothes to a man, and to a woman no more than a dress she no longer wishes to wear. You will not care one whit whether it is cremated, buried or dumped into the ocean."

CHAPTER 7

MORE ON THE EXPERIENCE OF DYING

As Delight promised she brought from her consciousness into mine further details on the experience of dying. I will set out this material for you in this chapter and give it to you in as orderly a fashion as I can. It seems that there are four points in relation to the experience of dying which should be dealt with in some depth:

1. The New Body of the Soul Following Death

The new body which the soul inhabits following its leaving of the physical body is most commonly called the "Astral" body. Some call it the "Mind" and/or "Mental" body. This is the body in which the SELF (Soul) houses itself immediately upon leaving the physical body. This new body contains the essence (consciousness) of the individual uninterrupted and complete as it was in physical life. Sometimes the emergence of the soul from the physical body occurs so naturally that it comes as a shock of surprise to the individual to find that he or she now inhabits a new type of body. Mostly however the experience is recognized.

If the astral body were to be described in the scientific terms of physics it could be said that it is composed of a most tenuous condition of matter existing at a highly accelerated rate of vibration to that of the condition of matter in the physical universe. The rate of vibration of this body is so rapid as to be imperceptible to normal sensing.

When the soul first enters its astral body form, having just left the physical, it experiences a bewildering effect as its new body seems more restricted than the form just left. It cannot move physical things. It cannot be seen or heard by those still in the physical body. It seems limited in what it can do in the physical world.[3] Actually this seeming

---

[3]What happens following the death experience is that one is in a sort of half-and-half position between the physical state of being and the astral state of being; the disembodied soul will soon enter a mental and/or spirit realm and leave the physical behind for a while. At the time of death, when first experiencing being out-of-body, this betwixt-between state can produce a confusing sense of perception for the individual.

limitation in relation to the physical world is to be expected and is a product of not yet fully understanding the new form in which one's consciousness is now housed.

To understand this, consider for a moment how it would seem to your observation of yourself if you had lived your life in a two-dimensional world and then suddenly emerged as a three-dimensional being. From your new point of view, things would seem bewildering and unfamiliar as long as you remained in a two-dimensional setting. However, once your new form enters into a three-dimensional realm then the advancement becomes obvious. You recognize that you have added an extra dimension to your state of being and now have greater freedom than you had before.

So it is with the newly formed astral body. You have - following death - added a new dimension to your being. Seen while still in relation to the three-dimensional world, it appears limited. You cannot do some of the things which were everyday experiences to you before but soon you will recognize that your new body is as far ahead of your old body as was the three-dimensional body over the hypothetical two-dimensional one. Such increased dimensional scope has fascinating potentialities for now you can pass through physical matter. So be not dismayed by the new body in which you find yourself following dying. Just relax. Accept it as natural to your new state of being. Get used to it gradually. Soon you will be delighted with the "form of formlessness" you now wear, at the new sense of freedom which you now experience at not being bound so tightly within a three-dimensional body as you were before.

2. Meeting Your Guide Following Death

Who is the "warm spirit" you will meet following death? Who will come to aid you in your passing over? This is a question to be asked only from this side of life. When the time comes for your "passing over", you will know who the guide is. You have known all your life.

People of all ages who are sensitive to such things have recognized that "something" or "someone" watches over them, something which is beyond themselves. Some refer to this as the teacher, some as a guardian angel - often described as a guide in the form of a brightly shining visage. There is nothing supernatural about angels. Angels are souls who have evolved beyond the need for the rebirth cycle back into the physical world. Some refer to them as the "hosts of God" and convey His positive principles of love and worthy attributes basic to Existence. Angels are expressed as having spiritual bodies which appear as "shining countenances".

What is a "guardian angel"? Search inside yourself and you will know, for it has been a friend with you all your life on this earth: a figure, being, entity, the still small voice within - call it what you will - that has, as its assignment, yourself. You and this Being have a close rapport. From my personal experience I know my own guide intimately. I can recall talking to it in my mind way back in my earliest childhood.

Possibly some will not choose to take this "guardian angel" concept seriously - whatever you wish. When you die you will know this Being intimately. There will be a natural warmth between you. Accept the friendship and let the guide aid you in your experiences following death.

3. Experiencing the Reveries

The "reveries", often as directed by your "guide" when passing over, are a review of your life, so that you can face up squarely to how you have lived and can prepare for a catharsis which you will shortly experience within the Shadowland. Just follow your guide on this and consider it an opportunity of learning.

You will recognize many mistakes you have made during the past life and see many things you could have done better, but no one is going to criticize you for them. If you are wise you will profit from them. Really there is a great opportunity afforded in passing through the process of death. It is a time of learning, of soul-searching and, if used constructively, of great advancement. If you are alert to its value it can be a tremendous experience but honestly most are so "asleep" that they only get confused by this review of their life and learn very little. The guide will help you in every way if you accept this help.

4. What is the Veil?

The "Veil" stands as one of the great esoteric mysteries of all time. The ancients likened it to a still river which you crossed from the shore of one world to the shore of another. Persons who have returned from near death experiences report it in various ways - as a sort of barrier, a grey mist, the doorway between earthly life and the next life. Whatever the imagery of the Veil, all concur that once passed through there is no returning to the body recently left. That incarnation is complete.

As to what the Veil is, it can best be likened as a place and yet not a place where the borders of two worlds (Existences) of different frequencies meet and cancel each other out. On the one side of this "doorway" lies the physical world, and on the other - bordered by the' reflective Shadowland - is the astral world and/or mind-world.

Is all this real or just imagination for the onward-passing soul? **It is assuredly experience and what more can you say about reality than that it is experience.** Man is so devoted to placing everything in spatial relationships that it is difficult for him to consider anything unless it is "somewhere". If the Veil must be conceived as being placed somewhere, place it as being universally close to everyone whatever the position in space as it will be experienced following death.

It is through this Veil that one passes in the astral body during the experiences of both birth and death. It is the Veil which divides one side from the other, and at birth hangs like a "curtain of forgetfulness" on the individual in the physical world. There is wisdom in this fact, for in the forgetting of past lives the immediate one is given precedence for full living. There is no need for a mystical explanation of this amnesia effect. Nature does not operate in supernatural ways but always in accordance with her laws, even if some are surprising.

The memories of past lives remain buried within the subconscious of each person, and by probing can sometimes be recalled. "Awakened Ones" can remember their births and deaths without interruption, such as Krishna's remembering which he describes to his disciple,

Arjuna, in the <u>Bhagavad-Gita</u>, iv. 5: "Many lives, Arjuna, you and I have lived. I remember them all, but thou dost not". In unenlightened man, the "curtain" is not lifted (except by special techniques) from the mind until death frees it and permits an expansion of consciousness.

When you look at it objectively the experience of dying is a wonderful one. Oriental people seem to understand this better than do most in the Occident. Death must be looked upon as being simply a time of transition from the human plane of consciousness to a higher (transcendental) plane of consciousness, and it should be accompanied by solemn joyousness as the climax of the life just lived.

Delight expressed it like this: "Truly if you will look upon death as a gift package you have been waiting for and expecting all of your life, when it comes you will receive it with gladness rather than sadness."

CHAPTER 8

WITHIN THE BARDO

In this chapter I will continue with my personal notations on various life after death matters which Delight channelled through to me. Accordingly we will now consider that which Delight refers to as the "Shadowland" - the space without space which lies between the physical world and the mind-world, the place in which the soul is given catharsis prior to its decision to return to the physical plane or to remain in the spiritual. This realm has been instinctively recognized by Man since time immemorial. In the Orient it is mostly known by the Tibetan term of "Bardo", and it is written of in this manner in the ancient Tibetan Book of the Dead:

"Regard this life, and the life between in the Bardo, and the next life, and accustom thyself to them thus, as one. And remember, blessed one, the light you will see within the Bardo is the radiance and reflection upon your soul of the light of the Godhead."

In relation to your complete understanding of the phenomenon of death it is important that you have a sort of overall picture of the "Bardo" concept. The way it is presented in the original work is so wrapped up in the mystical symbolism of the East as to be largely beyond the comprehension of Western people, so I will devote a personal chapter to it based upon my careful reflections on this matter which have developed since Delight spiritually called my attention to this soul-searching realm.

The true title of the immortal Tibetan Book of the Dead is Bardo Todol. The entire work deals with what the soul will experience within the Bardo - its purging, its choice for new life, and its rebirth again into the physical world. Any near death experience can only take one up to the Veil and no further. Only direct penetration of the transcendental can take one beyond the Veil and bring that information back to the living on earth. In the Bardo Todol, this is told:

There are two ways to consider the Bardo. One way is from Tibet, the other is from India. As we have spoken of the new body of the soul as being the astral body and that its destination is to return to its own realm, which we shall call the "astral world", I will discuss this first with the Eastern Indian concept. I will then give you the processes which the <u>Bardo Todol</u> says the soul will experience within the Bardo. It is well that you have both these insights; otherwise you could get hopelessly lost in the mystical symbolism of Tibet.

India's practice of Yoga affords an opportunity to explore the astral world (the astral plane) which the Yogi says is the realm of the soul. It is spoken of thus: the astral world coexists alongside the physical world, each occupying the same space and interacting with the other, yet in no manner interfering with each other. It is a law of physics that no two bodies of matter can occupy the same space at the same time. This is true within the range of the gross vibrations that make up physical matter but has no meaning whatsoever to that which exists beyond the limited range of such vibrations.

Within a set range of vibrations of energy are certain varying planes of Existence. The Yogi recognizes that there are countless such planes in the universal cosmos, and terms a group of these the "astral" world, as having special meaning to disembodied souls just as the "physical" world has special meaning to embodied souls. Now it must be understood that a **plane**, in the sense the Yogi uses it in relation to the astral world, is not a place of being - it is a **State** of being. "Astral plane" is an all-inclusive term applying to a great series of planes (states of being) immediately above those of the physical world, and rising upwards in gradually ascending scale to higher and yet higher states of spiritual planes or spiritual states of being. It is to the lower strata of the astral plane that the soul first goes upon passing through the Veil, and within this realm (in this state of being) it drops into a deep sleep, and within this state dreams occur which provide a catharsis to the soul, a complete cleansing. This dreaming will be good or bad as need be for its cleansing. Now it has been said that "dreams are real to the dreamer", while they last and this is true. To the sleeping soul what it experiences will seem just as real as any experience has ever been. Yet the truth is that they are self-induced from within the depths of the mind, for the soul still carries all that we call "mind" (memories, etc.) within itself. What will be experienced can be painful or delightful but whatever is experienced will ultimately pass, since it is Nature's way of deep catharsis for the individual involved.

The Bardo is the realm of the lower astral planes where the soul is purged, and this cleansing process follows a certain pattern in relation to the awareness of the soul. Understanding this you can understand the Bardo as it is presented in the <u>Tibetan Book of the Dead</u>, which is a graphic presentation of how this process appears to the individual (Soul and/or Self) on passing through the Veil. This is from the <u>Bardo Todol</u>:

"As you pass through the Veil and enter the Bardo realm it will seem to your sensing as a dimly lit grey world. Yet the light though dim is clear and you can see well for the realm is lit by the astral light.

"You have entered the shadowy borderland of the next world. It is a place of judgment, reflection and contemplation for the soul. Further it is a place for decision to advance rapidly to higher planes or states of being or to seek rebirth for shortly re-entering the physical world. The choice will be yours but first you will stand before judgment of your SELF as revealed within the 'Clear Light'.

"Soon you will see it and stand before it, within the Bardo, what is called the 'Primary Clear Light'. It shines with a great brilliance yet does not blind your eyes. At first you will tremble before it as its purity is devastating but soon you will take comfort in it.

"What this 'Primary Clear Light' is you will decide depending on your mental interpretation, for your mind is yours inclusive of your complete individuality in this realm as it was in the physical world. Thus you will not fail to rationalize what this 'Light' is. To some it is looked upon as God and will take on the form most religiously appealing to the soul. To the Christian it can be taken as the Christ, to the Buddhist that of the Buddha and to the Moslem the form of the Prophet, while yet others will contemplate it as the brilliance of their own soul, for the soul when recognized is the reality of SELF.

"As you stand bathed in the 'Primary Clear Light', now comes your opportunity for obtaining purity through a cleansing far more thorough than that which you underwent with your guide prior to entering the Bardo, which was a review of your past life experiences by way of preparation for what you are now experiencing. There is no mere reviewing of episodes of your life here. Now you will truly learn your real SELF; you will see your SELF and the way you have lived with an ablazed consciousness which presents the total impression of your life. And the judgment will then begin.

"It is not a judgment as though you stood before some great magistrate. It is rather that you stand before your SELF and become your own incorruptible judge. The purely personal point of view deserts you and you see yourself not only as others see you but as the impersonal power of 'karma' sees you (karma being the oriental term for judgment of what you have done or not done, that should have been done or not done.) Your true status is revealed to your SELF, and during this time you come face to face with the consequences of your actions in body and how your acts in the physical world have affected Existence. Have you raised Existence or lowered Existence? You will come to know the truth of your actions. It is a great soul-searching period, a period of much learning, a period of real growing up. If your deeds have been evil, a great remorse will fill you. If you have done well, you will benefit. You will come to see your entire life in complete perspective for what it was. All pretence is now gone.

"A wonderful opportunity is afforded while you stand bathed in the 'Primary Clear Light' for, if at that time you can come to a recognition of your Selfhood and Oneness with Existence, supreme insight and illumination will come to you. You will experience the radiance of the Clear Light of Pure Reality, and your spiritual emancipation may be gained instantly. The Sages refer to this as taking the 'Upward Path' in which faith is the first step, then comes illumination and with it certainty and when the goal is achieved, Emancipation! and a joining with the 'Hosts of God' is won.

"The period of your bathing in the 'Primary Clear Light' will last about an hour although, to the one experiencing it, it will seem timeless and all the while your guide will be standing by to aid you and help you understand what you are experiencing. Those of sufficient awareness will recognize the truth and win instant liberation, but most will not, sinking into a resting time to be awakened bathed in the 'Secondary Clear Light' of the Bardo.

"The 'Secondary Clear Light' is bright but not as bright as the first, and the call this time is for entrance into a higher spiritual state beyond the Bardo, as a pause for a time on a plane of Existence which has been called the 'mind world'; the 'heaven' of the Christian. If your karma is good and you are ready for it you can now pass beyond the Bardo and enter this higher spiritual plane and remain there for a time until the call for optional rebirth comes upon you. The principle is like the bouncing of a ball which reaches its greatest height at the first bounce, then the second bounce is lower and each succeeding bounce is still lower, until the ball comes to rest. So it is with the 'consciousness-principle' at the death of a human body. Its first spiritual bounce, directly upon quitting the earthplane, is the highest, the next is lower. Finally the force of karma having spent itself in the after-death state, the 'consciousness-principle' comes to rest, a womb is entered and then comes rebirth again into the physical world."

Oriental scholars who have studied the afterlife say there are three stages within the Bardo which follow the happenings of death. The first is known as the **Chikhai Bardo** in which the "Primary Clear Light" is perceived by the soul, and subsequently the "Secondary Clear Light".

The second state is known as the **Choyyid Bardo** and deals with the period (stage of being) following the appearance of the primary and secondary clear light in which many karmic hallucinations appear from out of the depths of the subconscious of the individual for the purpose of purging the soul prior to its rebirth.

The third stage is known as the **Sidpa Bardo** and is concerned with the onset of the birth insight and the entering again into the physical (from the formless back again into form), as a new incarnation in-body begins.

It may be said that there are three courses open to a soul within the Bardo:

1. Those of high spiritual evolvement who are awakened to their reality (enlightenment) have an opportunity to break the cycle of rebirth back into the physical and remain in the spiritual realm. Buddha calls this "Nirvana".

2. Those of spiritual understanding but with the desire still to be fulfilled in the physical, while appreciating the meaning of the "Clear Light", will follow their guide bypassing the Bardo and enter into the mind-world for a time until desire arises for yet another life in the physical world.[4]

3. Those of low spiritual natures who have shown poor karma in the physical world will find the purging Bardo experiences placed upon them disturbing, as is Nature's way. They experience little in the way of personal choice at this point, for this is the nature of the Bardo. Others of higher natures will find it reflective and revealing. The truth is this - the higher one advances spiritually and understands the basic reality of his or her true SELF the more self-control will be experienced within the Bardo. Those of low spiritual natures will never leave the Bardo realms but will remain therein for a time of cleansing and then, depending upon the strength of their desire to resume physical form, will enter rebirth shortly. Oriental scholars say this period can be for a time ranging from three to forty-nine days between death and rebirth to quickly resume karmic experiences in the physical world, for such a soul has many lessons yet to learn.

It is to those in this third grouping that the Bardo experiences of "karmic hallucinations" will then occur. It is a time of dreams, many of which reach nightmarish proportions. It is a time of cleansing in which are brought forth what Freud would call "monsters from the Id". It would not be amiss to liken this period, as experienced by the soul, to the conceptual "hell" of the Christian. But it is not a "hell" of endless suffering, burning in fire, eternal damnation or anything of that nature. It is not a "hell" into which any god plunges you or in

---

[4]Returning to the physical world means returning to physical form in three-dimensional space. It does not necessarily mean returning in form on the planet Earth (although many do so), as there are many planets in the vast universe capable of sustaining life in humanoid form. In its progressive reincarnations the soul will instinctively seek places of being which will contribute most to its growth.

which a devil makes you suffer. Existence is not against you. Indeed if you have the good sense to flow along with it and not struggle against it, these experiences of the Choyyid Bardo can be fascinating and decidedly worthwhile. Remember, Existence itself is completely neutral, and whatever suffering you experience at this stage within the Bardo is entirely of your own making. Actually it is a "burning up" of the inner karmic refuse, ultimately benefitting the soul before the next rebirth is entered for further physical world experiences in development.

Frequently Western theology is inclined to impose limitations on its understanding of this truth by refusing to take into account the esoteric in Christian traditions. Even the karmic hallucinations from one's subconscious can be met with understanding and, if you accept them, as lessons for yourself - many will even be pleasant. However, pleasant or unpleasant, as subjective experiences none will cause you harm. Just bear in mind that what comes forth is from within yourself. It is well that it is brought forth and is occurring to aid your ultimate advancement. So don't fight against what you experience; rather move along with your experiences and accept them with an understanding that, being entirely conjured up from your mind, they are now being purged from your subconscious.

From Delight, this . . .

"No matter how you find the Shadowland (Bardo), fear it not. It will cause you no harm of itself. Only you can turn it into harm against yourself. Understand that all have the same opportunity of reaching the same Divinity. It is God's gift to you; you have but to accept the gift.

"Just be passive about the hallucinations. If you are able, look at them objectively, as a witness. Flow along with whatever you seem to be experiencing. This is the most comfortable way of passing through the **Choyyid Bardo**. Indeed look upon the visions with interest and learn from the visions. Some will even give you a chance to perceive the world's materiality for the fundamental illusion that it is. If you can look upon your experiences in this phase of the Bardo with perception, you will gain a spiritual profit which will show itself in your following incarnation. Most, however, pass through the experiences in fearful dread. As asleep in death as they were in life, they gain little and do not avail themselves of this great opportunity for coming to know the truth that, while one's Existence now seems like a dream, it was always like a dream.[5]

"Let us now consider the **Sidpa Bardo**, which is devoted to the rebirth of the soul. After its session of hallucinating in the Choyyid Bardo the soul will arouse itself with an intense longing to seek rebirth into the physical world, ready to enter a human womb. The process is a conscious one by the soul which, if it is sufficiently aware, may even be selective as to whom its next parents will be. It is time to assume a new body, to return from the formless back into form."

As the Tibetans express it, at this time the body of the past life (the astral counterpart of what you are still wearing) will become more and more dim and the body of the future life will become more and more clear. The light of the "Six Sangsaric Lokas" will shine down and you will know, as though by insight, the place where you are to be reborn. At this time your body will partake of the colour and light of the place wherein you are to be born again. Visions of men and women in sexual union will appear before you and you will begin to wander to the doors of wombs. You will have the impression that you are either ascending, moving along on a level or going downwards. You are responding to the forces in the Bardo which tend to lead the deceased back to birth. These are the indications that you are wandering about in the **Sidpa Bardo**. It is at this time that you must form one single resolve in your mind. This is the important moment for firm resolution, and whatever you desire will come to pass and you can enter the womb of your choice.

The foregoing is how the process of rebirth will be experienced by the soul as it is described in the Bardo Todol.

Delight brings this insight:

---

[5]The closest Western theology has come to the idea of the Bardo is the purgatory concept, but the Bardo is not a "place" from which the soul may be prayed by another. Only SELF can remove itself from the Bardo. Some cling to the Bardo but for most the choice is made and the Bardo is quitted.

"Parents, know that you are in no sense the ruler of the child you bring into the world any more than the child is ruler of you. **Your child is a free soul even as you are a free soul, for freedom - freedom of will - is your very gift of Divinity from and/or with Existence and it may be that the soul within your child is a soul of far greater age - of far more rebirths - and wisdom than yourselves.**

"Mother, father, brother, sister, relatives, all remember this truth. Other than the bloodline which transmits physical body characteristics, there is no other relationship among you. True, family units and social ties can develop kinship, and proximity can bring about affection and love . . . but as for the soul which exists within the related body, each member of the family can be as different as north is from south. This truth is beautifully expressed by Gibran in this poetic form:

> 'Your children are not your children.
> They are the sons and daughters of Life's longing for itself.
> They come through you but not from you.
> And though they are with you yet they belong not to you.
> You may give them your love but not your thoughts,
> For they have their own thoughts.
> You may house their bodies but not their souls,
> For their souls dwell in the house of tomorrow,
> Which you cannot visit, not even in your dreams.
> You may strive to be like them,
> But seek not to make them like you.
> For life goes not backward nor tarries with yesterday.
> You are the bows from which your children as living arrows are sent forth.
> The archer seeks the mark upon the path of the infinite,
> And He bends you with His might that His arrows may go swift and far.
> Let your bending in the Archer's hand be for gladness;
> For even as He loves the arrow that flies, so He loves
> Also the bow that is stable.'

"All that parents can provide in a heredity line is the body (that which is physical). It is the soul which lives within that body that provides the heredity line of itself and has permanently stored within its Being all that it has ever been. This is the inner SELF which manipulates and motivates the body. It has been given - at first feebly and then with increasing strength.

"At the time of rebirth, should there be a miscarriage, abortion or other cause for the newly forming physical body to be rejected, fear it not. In truth, that which is immortal has nothing to fear ever. Existence will cause you no harm for you are part of Itself. Should you find yourself out of body again as a freed soul, simply re-enter the **Sidpa Bardo** for the selecting of yet another womb for rebirth.

"Safe within the womb the process is completed: spirit/mind (soul) fuses with the physical. The curtain of forgetfulness then descends upon all but the most enlightened, and when the time is due you will again be born into the physical world in your new three-dimensional body. Another incarnation of physical life for you begins anew."

To all of which the consciousness of Delight rings: "Amen!" - meaning "so it is".

CHAPTER 9

THE MIND-WORLD

As she currently is an inhabitant of the mind-world, I asked Delight to tell of that realm of Existence in some depth. She lovingly obliged:

"Immediately following death, and for a time thereafter, the soul is encased in its astral body form. Tenuous though this is it is still encasement. On entering the higher planes of the mind-world, this encasement drops, and the soul emerges in its mind-body. It is a lovely state, as it can now create its own form to appear to its consciousness as it wishes. Usually this is as one sees itself with the mind while in the physical body. The preferred image of oneself is the one which is assumed.

"**Indeed the creation by mind of what it desires to appear to the consciousness is a major characteristic of this realm**. That is why I have named it the mind-world, for it is a world so malleable to the mind. What may be experienced here by the SELF is only limited by what mind has the capacity to create in its immediate state of evolvement. To the Christian who holds ideas of Heaven having golden streets and palaces, it can appear so. To the Moslem who thinks of his Heaven as a place of wine, women and song, it can appear so. For most it will appear as their consciousness has experienced pleasures in the physical world. Whatever one's consciousness enjoyed most to have as its environment can be found here. What was recognized as most desirable in life in the physical world will be found here, for the mind-world is patterned, through mind, on the physical world.

"Lest it seem from this description that the mind-world is a world of imagination and/or a world of dreams, who is to say where imagination stops and reality begins? Often it has been expressed by men of deep thought that Existence is a dream within the dreams of the dreamer. There is no way that we can claim or disclaim this concept as right or wrong, since we know from experience that when we are caught up in a dream it presents an equal reality (at the time of the dreaming).

"However, let us 'assume' that the physical world is a reality unto itself, and the dream-world theory is a reflection of a glimmer of what is reality on the other side. For within the mind-world you will be living in an internal world of mental creation, yet it will seem to you as an external world, operating efficiently, and following patterns close to those you have been familiar with in the physical world. Who is to say it is not an external world as surely as the physical world, for the earthly world now left behind is a form of consciousness, as is the mind-world? As a form of consciousness it does not of necessity have to be a place, for the mind is entirely unbound by time and space. Yet the familiar feelings of Existence in relation to time and placement will be with you always on each side of the Veil. **That is the pattern of creation**.

"To understand this, appreciate that everything in the Universe has a positive and negative aspect. There is what may be called the 'inside/outside' effect - everything having its opposite. In relation to the pattern of creation the physical world in the positive aspect of creation is the product of the negative aspect of creation - which is the creative side, the mind-world side. The physical world and the mind-world are like the two sides of a coin, both being really only one, just different aspects of the same - **different consciousness views**.

"I would have you further consider the pattern of creation as the two sides of the coin, in a criss-crossing back and forth from one side of the Veil (which is the meeting point between the two sides) to the other. Thus you live for a time in body and thus you live for a time as freed mind and spiral ever upwards in relation to your advancing awareness (Enlightenment) of your true place in Existence.

"In this 'two sides of the same coin' is symbolized a proper understanding of the physical reality of space and the dream reality beyond space; the latter is a world of freed mind unshackled and unchained. In this note that what we know as physical is but a manifestation of mind as it expresses itself by the indirect process of physical manipulation while appreciating how much more God-like is the direct operation of the mind.

"From the psychological standpoint Existence in the mind world finds a close analogy in the states of sleep and dreams with which all are intimately familiar. Sleep is no more a stranger to the individual in the mind-world than it is in the physical, and much time will be spent in it for energy renewal by the soul. During periods of sleep the loss of consciousness will be the same in the mind-world as in the physical world - a succession of periods of remembering and periods of not remembering. Your consciousness has ever been a series of flashes of awareness. In like manner will you find your experience with consciousness in the mind-world, but there is a difference. The curtain of forgetfulness will have lifted from your mind in this realm of freed mind, and your awareness and capacity for experiencing can draw from the memories and associations of all your past lives rather than solely from the one immediately lived.

"Eastern teaching says it well. It is written along these lines . . . 'The master secret to understanding the psychological experience of death is to keep in view its identity with dreams and sleep. Mind is linked with the soul (SELF) and the soul is immortal. Thus mind/soul remains untouched despite the body's dissolution. We have no more reason to fear death than we fear sleep when we retire at night.'

"The psychological analogy of dreams continues into the mind-world, offering boundless capacities because your dreams in this realm are free of physical restraint. In dreams you can waft yourself from India to the North Pole or sail away on a summer sea to the islands of the Pacific or experience the heaven of your choosing. Conversely you can dream things of evil nature, for no realm is entirely free of this factor of Existence. But, as your karma has been cleansed in the 'Clear Light of the Bardo', you will find, figuratively speaking, that good may predominate in this world just as evil may predominate in the physical, yet there is good and ungood in each.

"The dreams you will experience in this world of mind are not the dreams of the confined mind in a physical brain which are usually of short duration and often of a wildness and illogical disorder. As a freed mind the dreams are presented to the SELF in a logical and reasonable order, are not limited by time and will seem as real and sensuously vivid as have any experiences you have had in the physical world.

"Your life in the mind-world will be in a far more private world than was your privilege when you were living in the physical and shared it in common with many other human beings. Your mind is a sanctuary of privacy and thus you will find it - alone in the aloneness of your own individuality. But being alone is not the same as being lonely - you are alone only in the sense that a dreamer is alone when he dreams. In this you will understand that the soul is in a private world of its own making but then we are not entirely strangers to this aloneness in a private world in the physical side of life either. We communicate with others. We meet in groups. We socialize. Yet the real SELF is alone inside each body very much in its own private world. We would hate any invasion of that privacy.

"Your dream existence in the mind-world is wonderful, as you fulfil personal yearnings and idealistic aspirations in a way that your past earth-life found impossible. Assuredly friends and loved ones who have passed over before will come to you. Remarkably the coming together will be experienced as within a dream. However it will be more intimate than was ever possible in the physical realm, as now there is a sharing of the dreams of each with the other. If there is a loved one or a beloved you seek, you will be brought together as each enters the 'soul dream of the other', a union in every sense as felicitous and blissfully spontaneous as the most idealized relationship in the physical world.

"I relate life to you in the mind-world in a simile to dream states for your ready comprehension of its reality, not to conjure ideas that life in the mind-world is not real. **All reality is as it comes to consciousness, and life as experienced in the astral is every bit as real as the reality experienced in the physical**. The world in which you find yourself beyond death will seem more plastic to your will than does the physical world in which you are confined in form. That is all. The mind has a greater direct control over forming your reality in this realm.

"Life within the mind-world with its experiences and meetings in the heavenly state is satisfying in every way for in the expanded consciousness of which the freed mind is capable, the fragrance of affectionate communications and beautiful interchanges of thoughts and feelings lingers long. The period spent in the mind-world is truly joyous and likewise the creativity of thought can operate now on a level largely unhindered.

"The importance of your lives in the physical world in relation to your lives in the mind-world (note that I say 'lives', not 'life', as you will live on both sides of the coin many times) will be obvious because of your affinity.

"Nature is efficient and since you have learned to live to good advantage in the physical world you will now live to good advantage in the mind-world. The converse is equally true. There are numerous advantages for a mind freed of bodily needs, since food is not needed to sustain it nor can illness affect it. Its energy levels are supplied directly from the infinite source with which the Cosmos is imbued.

"Truly the mind-world is a heavenly realm in which you are the master of your environment rather than being subject to it. The exquisite pleasures of living as a free mind are indescribable.

"In subsequent sessions of our conscious meeting I will tell you of some of these."

CHAPTER 10

MIND-WORLD GEOGRAPHY

Delight has channelled through a wealth of information regarding what is experiential beyond death, that which is known as the "Other Side". I have taken what she has given me and combined it with what other Enlightened Ones have expressed in the hope that I can give you these concepts in a clear manner for better understanding. In this chapter we will consider what may be called the geography of the mind-world.

In regard to the geography of the mind-world, it is more important to know **what you are** after death rather than **where you are** after death. Nonetheless it is interesting to have a conception of one's **where of being** as well as one's **what of being** in the hereafter.

It must be understood that the mind-world is not a place existing in space, as its dimensions are not those of space, but of vibrations. To understand better, encompass in this dimension the element of time, because vibration can only be measured by the rate of motion and that rate can be understood in the physical world only in terms of time. Examples are all around you to be appreciated, such as the vibrations (frequencies) that produce sound, light, heat, radio waves, etc. All these are measured in terms of time; i.e., so many vibrations to the second. The higher the rate of vibrations, the greater rate of speed manifested in the vibration.

Everything in the universe exists in accordance with its rate of vibration. It is so in the physical world; it is so in the mind-world, and each has its own range of frequencies. The substance of the astral plane (mind-world) is very much finer than that of the material plane (physical world), its vibrations being far higher than the finest forms of material substance (matter). In the mind-world there is a tremendous range of vibrational differences between its lowest and highest planes. In fact, the difference between the lowest planes of the astral and the highest planes of the physical is less than that difference. Indeed between these two extremes of astral vibrations there exists as great a range on the frequency scale as we have in the material world, but with this difference - the physical world is measured in space dimensions, while the mind-world is measured in vibrational dimensions. As you travel on the material plane you must traverse space (usually measured in accepted three-dimensional terms of length, width and height, or of feet, yards and miles, etc.), while on the astral plane when you must traverse rates of vibration, you pass from a higher rate of vibration to a lower or vice versa. **These various planes of vibratory energy constitute the geographical features of the mind-world.**

There are countless planes and subplanes (or "regions", which as far as consciousness is concerned are recognized as space and/or places of being) in the mind-world which may be travelled in relation to its geography by passing from one degree of vibration to another. Thus the geography of the mind-world will be seen as one of many planes and subplanes inhabited by souls fitted to dwell upon the particular plane most in accordance with their state of awareness in relation to the Universe. This coming to the consciousness as space to exist in is in every way as tangible as it was in the physical world.

Subtle principles of soul attraction draw each soul to the particular "region" for which it is suited. The universal law of attraction operates here unerringly. There is nothing haphazard about the process, nor is there anything mysterious about it. It is just the way it is. Nothing more, nothing less. The law operates with precision.

Each soul is restricted in its range by its own inherent limitations and degree of awareness (consciousness). The laws of nature on both sides of death are such that they must be followed. It is impossible for a disembodied soul to travel onto planes above its own immediate level. The laws of vibrational frequency prevent this. Conversely every soul, if it so elects, may freely visit the planes beneath its own and freely partake of Existence on those lower planes and mingle with the inhabitants thereof. This is a wise provision of universal law for, were it otherwise, the higher planes would be open to the influences of those dwelling on the lower planes. This nature does not allow as the higher planes are ones of greater refinement and purity.

Thus in the mind-world many advanced souls (higher consciousnesses) pass readily backwards and forwards among the lower planes bringing to the inhabitants joy, comfort and spiritual help. In this we find an understanding of the "guides", as certain of the more highly evolved souls are dedicated to the purpose of being guides and teachers to aid souls who seek such help in their development as well as to aid souls in making the transition of death. We surely are not strangers to this for many are the willing guides and teachers on earth who seek to aid in the advancement of humanity.

The geography of the mind-world will be seen to contain fully as many different kinds of regions as the physical world. Exactly as certain places in the physical world attract certain types of people (souls incarnate), so do various "places" in the mind-world attract certain types of entities (souls discarnate).

From Delight, this: "Such is Nature's way, or you may say God's way - whichever term is more meaningful for you."

CHAPTER 11

TIME IN THE TIMELESS

Some theories regarding life beyond death are expressed in vibrational terms, i.e. relating it to matter; from gross matter to matter of infinite fineness. They affirm that the higher its rate of vibration the higher the plane the soul exists upon and the more freedom it has. This is one way of looking at the astral plane and/or mind-world, and it is easy to understand, as we are familiar with it. However it can also be looked upon in terms of consciousness.

Consciousness is freedom. The more consciousness the soul has of its true Divine nature in relation to Existence, the more freedom it experiences. This is the transcendental point of view. From such a point of view let us speak of time in the realm beyond death.

Time in relation to the passing on of dear ones cannot be expressed more beautifully than to say it means putting the lamp away because it is dawn.

Time, as we know it by habit, is largely purposeful in the physical side of life. In the physical world, time is considered in essence as passing through a given space for a given period. In the mind-world, passage through space can be accomplished in a flash of thought. In this sense the beyond is timeless. Even in recognizing this truth it still must be appreciated that a "sense of time" has become so ingrained into our natures, been made so much a part of ourselves, that we have developed a psychological "time sense" in our subconscious which is as accurate as any watch. This "time sense" stays with us in the mind-world and while of no particular relevance is definitely heeded.

Time in relation to the matter of life after death can best be comprehended in the sense of looking upon the SELF itself - as opposed to its mental contents - as not being in time, and hence it is not limited to any successions of "before" and "after". Hence birth and death, which are ideas solely dependent on time, cannot apply to SELF. The soul, in this sense of not suffering limitations imposed by time, is immortal. Only in the pitiful illusions of those who do not appreciate the eternal nature of the Universe can it go out like a quenched flame.

Time beyond death is often spoken of in terms of eternity. Usually eternity is thought of in terms of endless time. It can also be considered as being the antithesis of time, meaning the exclusion of any kind of temporal relations. As Jesus expressed it: "There is eternity when you are not separated from God". Really eternity is timeless because it has no yesterdays or tomorrows. **It is always here and now**. Here and now eternally is the nature of the Universe, the nature of God.

In other words time is but an illusion of the mind in which it seems that there is past, present and future. The truth is there is only the present. The reality is that the future is never there for it is becoming the present, and from the present it is becoming the past. The only reality is the eternal present, the eternal NOW . . . there is no other than NOW. Live in the present and you live in eternity.

For all practical purposes, your use and understanding of time in the physical world will be parallel to its use and understanding in the mind-world. It is a convenience, that is all, for the truth is that it does not exist at all.

CHAPTER 12

AGE IN THE AGELESS

Ageing, as we know and experience it, is entirely a product of the physical world. It has no meaning whatsoever in the mindworld, as mind can conceive of itself as being of any age it desires. Age, as a product of the physical world, we observe largely through the vitality of the physical body which houses the soul. As the body becomes less useful, we refer to it as old age.

In the physical world emphasis is placed upon youth, and the ageing strive to look and act younger. There is no criticism in this. It is just how it it, but it is not in tune with reality, which is that in using up the body (its basic purpose is to be used up) you are really being brought just that much closer to the next new body to be used: in a spiralling upwards in evolvement. To become aware of this is to become aware of your own Divinity. Thus age is to be venerated. Somehow Oriental people have developed a culture recognizing this truth more than Western nations have.

Indeed age is to be venerated. Were this not so, life would be a great travesty and the ultimate of tragedies, for from the physical standpoint man goes downhill. We begin in the body as an infant that gradually matures to reach physical peak and then assuredly starts on the decline to eventual bodily uselessness. Occurring naturally, the body mechanism simply wears out and no longer functions as it did previously. Accident, disease or other causes prior to the wearing-out process of ageing merely bring the termination of the body's usefulness sooner. Happily, when the body is ready to be discarded, the soul can take its leave of the used-up body. In this, ageing is seen as only a self-made delusion of tragedy by the ignorant. For man is immortal and proceeds from the occupancy of one body to another during the process of the soul's evolvement.

It can be said that age in the mind-world is nonexistent, as there can be no wearing-out of that which is spiritual. **That is the meaning of immortality**. Being ageless the soul can exist in its consciousness in any bracket of age appearance that it desires. Its appearance is self-created as the individual wishes it to be. Mostly it seems that its choice of image is an appearance of vigorous young adulthood, based on preferred physical life images.

Pause for a moment and reflect upon how you know this is so. You will find that the appearance of the age you envision for yourself, inside yourself, has little bearing on the chronological passing of the years or how you look in the mirror. **It is as you see yourself within yourself.**

And directly from the consciousness of Delight comes this comment about age in the ageless:

"Let those who want youth rejoice that they are ageing, for in ageing they are just getting closer to youth anew."

CHAPTER 13

LOVE IN THE LIFE BEYOND

Those especially who deeply grieve the loss of a beloved one will seek an answer to the question: "Will we meet loved ones and friends who have died on the other side?" You have already been told of this, but since it has great meaning to every human heart, it will be well to elaborate more on the transcendental love in the life beyond death for those who enter the formless realm. Here is the essence of what Delight expressed on the matter:

"Heaven, even if it furnished every other joy, would not be heaven to the average person if it did not also furnish companionship and association with those loved in earth-life who have passed on before. The soul instinctively craves the society not only of those close to it by ties of love, such as man and woman, but also to those to which it is bound by the relationship of parent and child, brother and sister, friend and friend.

"This desire of the human heart has a wondrous realization in the mind-world. Not only do we know each other there, but we are naturally bound to those we have known in the physical world and also to others with whom we are in sympathy even though they are new to our experience. More than this, there is on the spiritual side the potential of a far closer companionship between kindred souls than earth-life affords. With the discarding of the sheath of the human body, the soul becomes capable of a closer relationship to others than it ever experienced on the physical plane, and new levels of love and friendship are achieved."

To appreciate what this means it is necessary to think of the highest ideals entertained in earth-life regarding relationships between human beings, for in the mind-world sentiments of love and friendship are idealized. On the physical plane such perfection of human relationships is seldom realized. In the mind-world it is the norm of behaviour. Those who are bound together by earth love have full opportunity to manifest their mutual affection.

The zenith of human imagination can only faintly scan the love that is possible between souls in love in the mind-world. Love blazes so brightly there that words can scarce express the truth. Of such love Whitman writes:

"As in a swoon, one instant,
Another sun, ineffable, full dazzles me,
And all the orbs I knew, and brighter, unknown orbs,
One instant of the future land, Heaven's land.
I cannot be awake, for
Nothing looks to me as it did before,
Or else I am awake for the first time,
And all before has been a mean sleep.
When I try to tell the best I find, I cannot;
My tongue is ineffectual, on its pivots,
My breath will not be obedient to its organs,
I become a dumb man."

The tremendous advancement of possible love in the mind-world over the physical world lies in the understanding - all over again - that the astral is not a place but a state. To dwell in the same place with a beloved is one thing; to dwell with a beloved in the same state of Being is another entirely. It can only be conceived in the idea of complete ONENESS OF TWO BEINGS!

Persons who have lost a loved one on earth frequently ask how they will find their beloved on the other side. The question would be more wisely phrased if they were to ask how can they NOT find their beloved - such souls attract each other like the opposite poles of a magnet and come together.

From Delight this:

"There is never any loneliness for souls who crave love and friendship in the mind-world. **Verily, there is nothing that is worthwhile and ennobling in earth-life that has not its magnified counterpart in astral-life.** The laws of nature operate fully in the mind-world just as they did in the physical world. The disembodied soul does not part with Nature in life beyond death, but rises to a phase of Nature which is fuller, richer and sweeter in every way. Only the one word - LOVE - can correctly express the real meaning and purpose of the heavenly planes on which is found love which 'casteth out all fear', blossoms in joy and bears fruit in peace."

CHAPTER 14

MONEY, MONEY, MONEY

"You can't take it with you" is decidedly true in relation to money. If you desire money strongly in the physical world it is one of the desires which will bring you back quickly again into the material plane, for the truth is that, while it occupies a very positive place of importance in the physical world, in the mind-world it has no importance at all. That is why Christ said: "It is as difficult for a rich man to enter the Kingdom of Heaven as it is for a camel to pass through the eye of a needle."

In the physical world acquiring wealth can have a purpose, but money accumulated just for itself is ridiculous. It is not even a good hobby. Money accumulated just for itself is decidedly sterile.

Money is sterile because it is only a symbol of value, not real value. It is not even especially pleasant to look at, or original or creative in form. It is based entirely on a physical world's speculatory evaluation which is so unsteady that its own value can't even be trusted from one day to the next. Money can be likened to the physical body with no spirit within it. When it dies it remains dead. It could be said that money has no opposite side to itself, as though it were "yang" without the "yin".[6] Little wonder it is sterile.

The only real value money has is in proportion to the usefulness of its application in the physical world. For so many however it becomes a useless end in itself. It is placed in the bank and not used for anything. Some even sew it up in a mattress. It is rationalized that its purpose is for the future, but the future is an illusion, so why waste a lifetime on acquiring that which is for the use of what may never occur? It can hardly be interpreted that people behaving in this way are showing much confidence in Existence.

---

[6]"Yin" and "yang" are oriental terms for the female and male factors in the Universe; the creative and the product; the negative and positive of Existence and/or Creation.

Actually money is one of the most common and mundane things you can find on earth and it is easy to acquire if you enter into the flow of it. If money is your wish, Existence will bring it in steadily. Jesus told this truth centuries ago when he said: "Seek first the things of the spirit and then all other things will be added to you". Jesus does not condemn wealth. He is simply saying that wealth does not even have to be sought. When you develop things of the spirit, any physical needs which money can bring to you will be an automatic process. Jesus is saying why waste your life in seeking that which is of so little real value when there are so many things of real value to seek.

The true status of money as seen from a transcendental position is that it has no real meaning in the mind-world other than as a fun thing, a game to be played.

What is the meaning of wealth in a realm where all that is wished for can be the direct creation of mind? Understand this deeply. What is the value of money which can be created in your mind on the instant? - such things, representative of wealth, become so commonplace as to lose all intrinsic value. Therein lies the truth - why waste a lifetime in acquiring that which adds so little value to your next life?

If making money in the physical world provides enjoyment for you, by all means make money. Existence is a playground. **Play as you wish in it**. If making money is your thing, to get the most fun out of it learn to use it wisely and as it leads to acquisitions let it lead to personal growth and the growth of others around you. If you can show that wisdom, then you can let what wealth you have be the means of bringing in higher values of progress and spirit.

On the matter of money, from Delight comes this:

"There is no harm in acquiring great wealth if you possess it rather than allowing it to possess you. Look upon wealth as a means of acquiring greater freedom to do that which is worthwhile doing. If you can handle money in that way, then it is worthwhile acquiring in the physical world, as the stewardship of fortune can teach many lessons worthy of learning, but for far too many it is simply money, money, money . . . jingle, jangle, jingle."

CHAPTER 15

TREASURES AND COLLECTABLES

Delight continued . . .

"Personal treasures and collectables which are dear to your heart are an entirely different matter from accumulating money just for the sake of it. Money of itself is sterile. Treasures and collectables are warm and rewarding.

"Collecting is such fun. Just remember that the treasures one collects in the physical world must be kept in their proper perspective, that's all. Their worth is actually directly related to the enjoyment they bring the collector. As always, understand that the Universe is meant for playing. Collecting is a form of playing. Keep it that way and enjoy. That is the only secret. If your treasures also prove a joy to others, so much the better.

"Do not think that the passing from form to formlessness mars the enjoyment of collectables in any way, for nothing that is collected which is really fine, beautiful and worthwhile is ever lost. As it is in the physical world, so it is in the mind-world.

"**For what is beauty but in the mind of the beholder, and what are interesting things but those which must hold the attention of the mind on that which is worthwhile.**

"A mind filled with that which is beautiful and interesting is a good mind. Remember, all you acquire and accumulate in the physical world which is lovely goes along with you in mind and spirit, and what you found of interest on one side of the coin you will find equally of interest on the opposite side, for it remains in your consciousness always.

"Worthwhile treasures are treasures wherever you are!"

CHAPTER 16

THE QUESTION OF KARMA

Karma has been mentioned at various times in this book. In the Orient karma is looked upon as a serious law of spiritual growth. Bad karma is presented as a deterrent to the growth of the soul, while good karma aids its growth. Simply put, karma is the worth of works. Karma will be seen as not expressing what you are, but what you have done to make you what you are. To expound a little: in the way of our living is found the way of developing karma, be it good or bad and, as our living is the result of our thoughts, we can say that all that we are is the result of what we have thought. It is founded in our thoughts; it is made up of our thoughts.

Some Oriental sects present very strict tenets with regard to karma, stating that if wicked deeds are performed in one lifetime they must be atoned for in the same or another lifetime. Further that if things are left incomplete in one life they must be completed in the next. On dying, the good or bad karma which a person has accumulated will affect their rebirth status - those with bad karma quickly reincarnating in the physical world again to complete what is yet to be completed and to atone for the karmic mistakes of previous Existence.

It will be noted in this karmic concept how closely allied it is to the Christian's belief of the person steeped in sin, who has not sought forgiveness from God, being condemned to hell. All such concepts of karma and sin are represented as deriving some judgment from some imperial god or by some strict law or universal code. All such presentations hold grains of truth within them but are so dramatized and personalized as to lose their true meaning. The Buddha, from his position of transcendental consciousness, gave a much more accurate view of karma, saying that nothing is to judge Man except himself; that to recognize his true Divinity he will have to cleanse and/or drop his karmas (which he refers to as "thought coverings"), of which there are three kinds:

The first, Buddha called "**karma averna**" - incomplete acts, stating simply that unfinished acts cover your Being, and each act wants to be completed as there is an intrinsic urge in everything to complete itself. Allowing some act to hang around incomplete, it covers you.

The second, Buddha called **"karma klesas"** - greed, hate, jealousies and things of such nature; these are impurities.

The third, Buddha called **"karma ghaya"** - beliefs, opinions, ideologies, judgments, preconceived ideas which do not allow you to grow nor allow awareness to enter. They don't even allow you to see clearly.

The Buddha did not present these as laws of judgment upon you, but simply as "thought coverings" which have to be discarded by those who wish enlightenment to come, an awareness of SELF to come. Karma is psychological in nature, as it is based on thoughts. Thought binds you in so many ways that it causes you to cling to things of the materialistic world and miss your Divinity. To name a few: if a man seeks wealth in a miserly sense, if he revels in personal gratification, if he selfishly aims to get what he wants in any manner no matter what the cost or how it hurts others, such a man, through his passionate attachments to things of the physical world, may be said to be acquiring bad karma. Conversely the man who puts self aside and devotes himself to doing deeds of kindness, may be said to be acquiring good karma. All such doings in life are rooted in the soil of thought, their seed in thought. Jesus tells it so perfectly: "As a man thinketh in his heart so is he."

Both Buddha and Christ tell you the truth about karma. Buddha speaks to the head via the intellect. Christ speaks to the heart via the emotions. Buddha is intellectual. Jesus has sentiment. Both are great!

As life is an over and over repeating of its form until awareness dawns, karma has become intimately associated with reincarnation. As thoughts of the type which Buddha refers to as "thought coverings" remain with the individual, buried within the subconscious, one lifetime can affect subsequent lifetimes. The stream of consciousness is actually continuous in the individual, although many are not sufficiently aware to recognize it. This can be revealed by psychological methods when skilfully applied by previous life regression techniques. Such previous life regressions can be used as psychotherapy and show how subconsciously buried experiences from a past life may remain with the individual and affect the current life, and they should be cleansed away. This throws a new light on the age old question of karma and shows how experiences of different lifetimes intermingle to affect and/or to make up the total individual.

Jesus has a way of solving the karma dilemma also in the very beautiful concept of repentance. Jesus says in effect to recognize your sins as mistakes you have committed and ask your Father in Heaven to forgive you. In doing this you will be forgiven. This is another way of saying judge yourself fairly and squarely and resolve to correct your errors. In recognizing your "Father in Heaven" you recognize your own Divinity, and thus sins and/or bad karma are cleansed.

In summary, karma will be seen as a psychological phenomenon which is intimately related to reincarnation; the non individual living life after life. While it does not affect the immortality of a person, it is a factor important to their worthwhileness in living, peacefulness of being and awareness of their Divinity. How better can the truth of karma be told than in this poem by an unknown writer:

> "Karma - all that total of a soul
> Which is the thing it did, the thought it had,
> The 'self' it wove with woof and viewless time
> Crossed on the warp invisible of acts.
>
> Before beginning, and without an end.
> As space eternal and as surety sure,
> Is fixed a Power divine which moves to good,
> Only its laws endure.
>
> That which ye sow, ye reap. See yonder fields.
> The sesamum was sesamum, the corn was corn.
> The silence and the darkness knew;
> So is man's fate born.
>
> He cometh, reaper of the things he sowed,
> Sesamum, corn, so much cast in past birth;
> And so much weed and poison stuff, which mar
> Him and the aching earth.

If he labour rightly, rooting these,
And planting wholesome seedlings where they grew,
Fruitful and fair and clean the ground shall be,
And rich the harvest due."[7]

From Delight comes this on karma in her wonderfully concise manner: **"Your karma will be as you feel it will be."**

---

[7]In this footnote I wish to amplify on the karma matter, as it is important to you. It is presented here with a lightness of handling rather than with the profoundness often customary. Karma to many seems an inexorable law of the Universe expressed in such sentiments as: "As ye sow so shall ye reap", "An eye for an eye and a tooth for a tooth", "The scales of justice must be balanced with justice". It is felt that whatsoever you have done in one lifetime which is harmful must be justified by your suffering through an atonement for it in a subsequent lifetime to work out the "bad karma", as it were.

Some even express the matter with such pessimism as to say that if what you did before in a life caused a thousand deaths, you must suffer a thousand times in your current one. This is an extreme example, but even those who do not believe in the concept of reincarnation hold ideas of judgment of the soul for its actions in this life on earth before its admission to happiness in the life which lies beyond death.

As insights from Delight bring in matters related to the questions of karma, all such conceptions miss the point - **as your Being is that you feel you are** - or as Jesus expressed it: "As a man thinketh in his heart, so is he". This is so even when Being is encased within the confines of the body (form) and it is amplified a hundredfold when in the formless - in the mind-world which, as you have learned to understand, manifests a level of heightened creative freedom.

Thus, if you go unto death holding ideas of a stern karma being the lot in the next life upon rebirth, you will most assuredly experience a stern karma. This is the way of mind, but not the way of Enlightenment (Truth) at all, which is why I have presented the matter of karma in the happier vein as a repentance of sins rather than as an inexorable justice for sins. You can make of karma a long, enduring hell if you wish, or you can drop it on the moment. The choice is yours.

CHAPTER 17

FROM THE FORMLESS INTO FORM

The determining factor of how long a soul will remain in the mind-world depends upon what its desires are. It may be for a considerable length of time, as it is an enjoyable stay, and in this delightful world you will enjoy all manner of happy events: children, adults, love, adventures, beauty, creativity - all manner of nice things which have meaning for you and which eventually fill your life.

Life in this realm is in every way worthwhile. You are in it as a person worthy of appreciating it, otherwise you would not be here at all. In every way you are uniquely yourself. As a soul remember always: YOU ARE YOU! Thus the experiences of living in the mind-world will be individual for each soul. You are no stranger to this, for your life in the physical world is equally unique and is of your own creation, but in the mind-world you will experience this as immensely more intimate and personal.

Your stay in the mind-world has no special termination time and is as your desires move you. In your state of freedom you have great choice. If your stay has resulted in spiritual advancement and that becomes your aim, you can rise up to yet higher planes of Existence into the spiritual realms of the astral. It may be that your desires will call you back for another incarnation in the physical world. Many souls respond to this call, for the link with the physical is strong. Mental ties exist that continue to feel the need of the physical body in which they were formed. Such souls are driven by their own forces sooner or later to return to earth again.

Often these ties or links with the physical world need a new incarnation for completion. All this can be expressed as being part of the evolution of the soul as it wishes such evolution. The individual is inwardly impelled to think in space/time characteristics which will bring the earth back into consciousness. At this time the soul will sink into a profound and dreamless sleep of resting from all burdens of personal consciousness. The peace and refreshment which you found intermittently for a few hours at a time in physical life is now enjoyed for a long, uninterrupted period.

From this "sleep" the soul will awaken to find itself within the Shadowland (Bardo) realm in search of rebirth, for the individual stream of mind flows in continual circulation through the incarnations and is not exhausted by any one of them. No life is a finished one. It is a continuum. Sexual union on the physical plane brings two cells together, which unite into a single growth, but it does not create new life. It merely creates the new condition in which an old life can express itself anew.

From Delight this:

"Rebirth is simply a renewing of that which was without form for some moments now in form again."

CHAPTER 18

REINCARNATION

The return of the formless into form is called reincarnation. Some believe in it, some do not. Belief or unbelief is irrelevant. It is the way of the Universe. Everything is patterned on birth, death, rebirth. The very stars, vast galaxies, follow this pattern. So accept this truth: **there is not a living person in the entire world who has not returned from death.**

We have all died many deaths before we came into this immediate incarnation. What we call birth is merely the reverse side of death, like one of the two sides of a coin or like a door which we call the "entrance" from the outside of a house and "exit" from the inside. The argument of a person that merely because he has no conscious memory of his many births and deaths proves that reincarnation is untrue is scientifically untenable. The field of man's perception, as it is easily demonstrated, is extremely limited. There are objects he cannot see, sounds he cannot hear, odours he cannot smell, tastes he cannot taste and feelings he cannot feel.

With the senses of the physical body so obviously limited, it is really astonishing that anyone should question the possibility of reincarnation just because he cannot remember his previous life and thus conclude that he has had no previous Existences, for in like manner no one remembers his recent birth, and yet no one doubts that he was born.

It was not so very many years ago that evolution was a theory believed in by a few. Today it is accepted by the majority. What is evolution but the evolvement of the physical body, while reincarnation is the evolvement of the soul? Both are concurrent and are interrelated. Body after body, or more properly expressed, life experience after life experience, must be engaged in for the growth of the soul.

In the Bible Christ says: "Except that a man be born again, he cannot enter the Kingdom of God". That is from the English translation, and Christian doctrine has interpreted "born again" as meaning a spiritual rebirth. The original Hebrew text however has it written as "born again and again". In the Koran it is written: "God generates beings and then sends them back over and over again till they return to Him".

Many of the world's greatest minds have given credence to reincarnation. Voltaire wrote: "After all, it is no more surprising to be born twice than it is to be born once. Everything in Nature is resurrection". Nietzsche states: "Live, so that thou mayest desire to live again - that is thy duty. For in any case, thou wilt live again!"

You can unravel the matter for yourself, if you reflect upon concepts which place as truth only one lifetime in the physical world which at the most rarely exceeds 90 years, and then balance it against an eternity on the other side. Such beliefs paint a very unbalanced picture of Nature indeed. Likewise the idea that one's behaviour during that minute "droplet of time" in the great ocean of Eternity determines one's status in relation to God for the remainder of each soul's Existence for the aeons which lie ahead is equally incongruous.

How long will the process of reincarnation continue for the soul? - for the "while" in which there is yet much to learn, much to desire and much to experience in the physical world. As long as the desires for the physical world are there, the soul will reincarnate. Yet the process is not endless. Eventually Enlightenment comes to every soul and the cycle of rebirths is broken.

The importance of reincarnation cannot be over-emphasized if a full comprehension of soul growth is to be understood. Incarnations in the physical world are experiences in which the soul is gradually burnished to become a thing of beauty. This is Enlightenment, which is a recognition of one's true SELF, one's true status in relation to Existence. It can take many, many lifetimes - in both the physical world and in the mind-world - for some to reach that realization. . . that realization that some call "Nirvana" and others "Oneness with God", and yet it is possible to achieve it this very moment. Birth and death are not phenomena which happen only once in any given human life. They occur uninterruptedly. At every moment something within us dies and something is reborn. The teaching of reincarnation is but an extension of this.

It is of great importance that the doctrine of reincarnation is today being given more and more credence by Western cultures, for when that long-awaited agreement among all people as to the truth of the matter occurs, there will no longer be doubt, no fallacious argumentation directed against this concept. Then will Occidental man awaken from the slumbers of ignorance which have been hypnotically induced by a mistaken orthodoxy and concur with his Eastern brother.

Here are the sentiments regarding reincarnation as expressed in the Hindu religious text, The Upanishads:

"As a man's desire is, so is his destiny. For as his desire is, so is his will, and as his will is, so is his deed, and as his deed is, so is his reward, whether good or bad. For a man acts according to the desires he treasures. After death he goes to the next world bearing in his mind the subtle impressions of these deeds and, after reaping the harvest of his deeds, he returns again to this world of action. Thus, he who still has the desires of the earth continues subject to rebirth. But he who has not earthly desires, who has discrimination, whose mind is steady and whose heart is pure, and who does not desire to be reborn, reaches the goal, and having reached it, is form no more, and remains amongst the hosts with God."

To which Delight says: "Amen!"

CHAPTER 19

THE QUESTION OF GOD

I asked Delight the ultimate questions: "Who is God? Where is God? What is God?" Smilingly she flooded my Being, so possibly I can write a little about God with a trace of wisdom.

God is the Mystery of Mysteries of the Universe. It is so on both sides of death. Death in no way solves the Mystery of God. From time immemorial Man has tried to solve this Mystery. This is why there have been so many names for God, so many sects, so many religions . . . each and every one of them trying to solve the Mystery of God; each and every one of them just Man's dreaming about how God is or how God must be.

The Mystery remains unsolved, which is the way it must always be, for if the Mystery is solved it will no longer be a Mystery. The truth is that, while you can experience God with your heart, you cannot solve the mystery of God with your head. If you will accept this you can move closer to an understanding of God and possibly some answers to your questions about God can be given - a little.

The moment one gets close to death one thinks of God. Those who have not prayed for years and years will pray when they are dying, for if anything is to save them from death it will have to be God. Since God is basic to our immortality it is well that we understand Him a little, even if that little has to be minimal.

Generally speaking the majority of Western religions present man and God in terms of duality. Man is here; God is there - usually placed in some distant situation conceived of as "Heaven". With such, the only possible path to God is a long one of hoping to reach God as a distant goal by pleading somehow for His attention, by prayers or by bribing Him with worship. To put it bluntly Western religions hold that Man is mortal and will only be granted Divinity (immortality) if it pleases God to grant it.

Eastern religions, generally speaking, present Man and God in a "oneness" relationship. In this oneness duality is bypassed and one approaches God on an equal basis. In this oneness, Man himself is recognized as the Divinity. God is seen as being within Man. When this is recognized, it is perceived that the SELF (soul) is immortal already, is unchanging, is and always has been. This has been beautifully expressed in a poem from the Hindu scriptures, The Gita:

> "Never the spirit was born;
> The spirit shall cease to be never.
> Never was time it was not;
> End and beginning are dreams.
> Birthless and deathless and changeless
> Remaineth the spirit forever;
> Death hath not touched it at all,
> Dead though the house of it seems."

Western religions are far more modest than are Eastern religions. Christianity, Mohammedanism, Judaism, etc., all separate man from God, presenting man as lowly and God as exalted. Christianity for example has Man represented as a sinning creature who has fallen from God's good grace, to which grace he can only be restored through the mercy of God. Eastern religions do not feel that way at all, but believe that man is under no sin - that he has only to awaken to his reality and recognize his true God-status in Existence - recognize his own Divinity, as it were.

The experiencing of the truth of God within is transcendental and has been expressed by all the great Masters who have told of God to Mankind from widely divergent parts of the world and down through the ages such as Christ, Buddha, Krishna, Lao Tzu . . . all have expressed the same Reality. One sage from the western part of the world was Heraclitus (540-480 B.C.), who lived in Greece during the time of Aristotle. Heraclitus expresses the truth about God in the Universe in this manner:

"This universe which is the same for all has not been made by any god or man, but it has always been, is, and will be - an ever-living fire, kindling itself by regular measures and going out by regular measures. The phases of fire are craving and satiety. The sun is new each day."

In this Heraclitus is removing a man created, named god or limitation of god from a human-like personality. The Chinese sage, Lao Tzu (6th Century B.C.), puts it this way in the very first chapter of his superlative book, <u>Tao Te Ching</u>, which has been translated more times than any other book except the Bible:

"The Tao that can be told is not the eternal Tao. The name that can be named is not the eternal name. The nameless is the beginning of heaven and earth."

The Tao is not a name for God. The Tao is simply a Chinese character which means "the way". In this, both Lao Tzu and Heraclitus echo each other in saying there is no god as a separate creator of the Universe and cannot be - **because the Creator and the Creation are one and the same**. Existence is one. Existence is the Isness. Existence, itself, is the Creator. It, itself, is the creativity. Heraclitus, like Lao Tzu and all the great Masters who have shown the way to God, is a non-dualist. A non-dualist is precisely opposite to the person who says that God is one thing and Man is another, or that God rules in some distant heaven and is deciding what should or should not be done with Man, to punish or reward. All Masters, both Eastern and Western, have expressed this truth of the non-duality of Existence (God).

Jesus says it very simply: "The Kingdom of God is within you". That is what is meant by ONENESS WITH GOD.

The human mind is tricky and, the moment it perceives anything, it inevitably divides. In relation to Creation, it says that for there to be a creation there has to be a creator. The mind won't let it drop even there, for then it says that, if there is a creator, then there must be a creator of the creator - creator A creating creator B, creator B creating creator C - and on and on endlessly. The Masters however all say this is nonsense; Creation is not duality - it is ONENESS.

Possibly you cannot see so far away, so let's bring it closer to home. Heraclitus says: ". . . craving and satiety . . .". On the surface these seem like two, but underneath they are not. You feel hunger, then you eat and then you feel satisfied. So it seems as though those are two different conditions but actually they are one, for food changes both. Food becomes the bridge between hunger and satiety, desire and lack of it. If they were really different they could not be bridged - hunger would remain hunger and satiety would remain satiety but the truth is they are not different. They are one.

Consider the very personal matter of life and death. Life and death seem so separate from each other - complete opposites. In truth they are not separate at all. They are one. Life is the manifestation of cosmic energy, and death is the relaxation into the same energy. Life is coming to form, and death is moving again into the formless. Life is not separate from death. Death is not separate from life. It is one phenomenon. Just as a new morning is a beginning of the evening, a new birth is a beginning of death. One helps to bring the other. If there is no morning there will be no evening. If there is no death, don't think there will be life eternal - there will be no life at all because death creates the situation for renewed life. Every life brings death. Every death brings life again.

The duality complex of the mind in relation to God is what has mixed the world up badly in understanding the Divine and it has been the cause for so many conflicting sects being created, so many names for God being coined by Man. Great theologians are equally deceived by the mind and say: "God created the world." This statement is juvenile. Nobody has created Existence. IT IS. It is simply there. Men like Lao Tzu, Heraclitus, Buddha and Zarathustra have penetrated the truth. They simply say: "Existence is God". Nobody has created it. There is no creator who is responsible for it, so don't raise unanswerable questions and don't waste your time in unnecessary answering. Accept it simply as God - the Mystery of Mysteries. Leave it at that!

The closest you can come is that Existence IS - and God is not separate from it. God is Existence; the Totality. It comes out of its own and dissolves. Heraclitus says: "It is fire". Fire is a beautiful symbol. It gives you a picture of a very dynamic energy; indicates that Existence is dynamic, dialectical energy which moves on its own. Call it Cosmic Energy if you like. Call it God if you like.

When you say "Cosmic Energy" (the energy of the Universe; the energy of Existence) it means something. When you say a named god, you have moved into something which will not lead anywhere except into conflict and confusion. Energy is the basic truth. You can feel it here and now. You are energy - the birds singing in the trees are energy - the trees growing towards the sky are energy - the stars moving - the sun rising every day - everything is energy. Energy is neither good nor bad. Energy is always neutral. There is no need for you to create a god, to name a god for yourself.

There is likewise no need for you to create a devil to explain away something which you feel is evil. If you are miserable it is because of yourself, not because of a god or a devil causing you misery. If you are miserable it indicates that you are behaving with the energy of the Universe in the wrong way. You will be happy if you move with the energy and don't struggle against it. If you will remember that there is no named god who is responsible for what happens, then you will appreciate that **you** are responsible - and then there is a possibility of recognizing your own Divinity. If a god or devil is responsible, then there is no possibility.

Named gods and devils are tricks of the mind to throw responsibility on somebody or something else, because the mind is always throwing responsibility on somebody or something else. If you are angry you may believe "someone else" has created the anger. If you are sad, "somebody" is making you sad. If you are frustrated, "somebody" is blocking your progress. The mind says that "somebody else" is responsible, not you. Thus you seem freed of the responsibility and that is why you are miserable.

Responsibility is yours, which is a fact that the experience of death will bring strongly home to you. As Jesus expressed it: "Responsibility is yours, says the Lord". When you recognize this, immediately you understand what Jesus meant when he said: "God is within you". Now you can look at the world through totally different "eyes" and know that if you feel miserable you have not taken responsibility for yourself.

That's all that "sin" means - that you have not taken responsibility for yourself and have not learned how to flow with the total energy system of Existence. Why blame sin or unhappiness on some imagined devil or satan? **Accept the responsibility of living yourself. Remember the energy system of Existence is neutral**. If you flow with it you will be happy. If you don't flow with it, you will be miserable. No named god or devil is responsible.

We create our conception of God out of our own fears and needs. We feel at times so helpless in our misery; so powerless and impotent in our pain. Out of this fear we create a god to whom we can pray, to whom we can say: "Don't give me so much trouble" or "Please take this trouble away from me". "I worship you, dear God, so please do this for me and, if you do, I promise to keep on worshipping you more and more". Towards such a god we feel that if we praise him then he will become more and more favourable to us. How do you feel about God? Do you think God can become prejudiced, and that if you pray He will be on your side and if you do not pray He will not be? We have created all named gods out of our need. Really it is your need because you feel you are helpless, and then you project onto him that you are helpless. If you are powerless, obviously you will say he is omnipotent. If you are ignorant, obviously you will say he is omniscient. Whatever you miss in yourself you will project onto him and then you think the balance is recovered and can say: "Now I can pray to this omnipotent, omniscient, omnipresent Being and He will be helping me". **When you recognize the truth that it is you who are responsible, that it is you who have the power to make all right, then it is that you will know that you are made in His image.**

If you feel other than that you are created in the image of God, you are being deceived by tricks of the mind. If you want to talk or pray to Existence/God, by all means talk - but remember your talk is not going to affect Existence. It may affect you (via auto-suggestion) and that may be good, but prayer is not going to change God's mind. There is nobody listening to you. This vast Cosmos cannot listen. However this vast Cosmos can be with you if you are with it. When you appreciate that you are an actual part of it, then you can pray to it and transform your reality into what you wish. Real prayer is a feeling, a flowing with Nature. Real prayer is a Cosmic energy phenomenon, not a devotee/god phenomenon. You simply become silent. You simply open yourself to Existence. You raise both your hands towards the heavens with your upturned face and feel Existence flowing into you. You become ONE. You merge with Existence. It is then that you know the Divinity in your Self.

Drink deep of this wisdom, for in it you discover your immortality. You can recognize your deathlessness while you are living in form. You can discover it equally while living out of form in the life beyond death.

From Delight this:

"Mystery of Mystery though the question of God is, in the continual game we play with Existence, perchance you will begin to get a glimmer of understanding of that mystery. You should, as God is your nature. If you would come to know God, come first to know yourself."

CHAPTER 20

SPIRIT COMMUNICATION

Among the people of the Orient there is not the slightest doubt that the dead can communicate with the living. "The dead communicating with the living" - what a misconception that is! How much more correct it is to say **the formless communication with those in form**. It can be done. It has been done many times. However it is not recommended by those of Enlightenment that it be done except by those of high spiritual evolvement.

In the Tibetan Book of the Dead it is cautioned against in this manner; recognize that there are malignant spirits of certain orders as well as good spirits. Recognize these malignant spirits for what they are and avoid them well, for they are "pretas" (unhappy spirits) and deceased human entities who, becoming habituated to the Bardo, have retarded their normal evolution. Such spirits have accepted the Bardo as their reality and make no attempt to leave it. On being called up, these spirits will give false counsel as to the real nature of the Bardo. They will describe the Afterlife in which they now dwell in terms of what they believed the nature of the Hereafter to be while still in the physical world.

For just as a dreamer on earth lives over again in his dreams the experiences of his waking state, so the inhabitant of the Bardo (which is pre-eminently the realm of illusion) experiences hallucinations in karmic accord with the contents of his consciousness created by the physical world. Thus it will be observed that none but very exceptional spirits when called forth have any rational philosophy to offer concerning the realm in which they exist. They are regarded as being merely playthings of karma, lacking mental coherence and stability of personality, more often than not being mere "psychic shells" which have been cast off by the consciousness-principle and which, when coming into rapport with a human "medium", are galvanized into automated actions.

As it is written in this Tibetan text: "Only the high spirits are to be evoked, such as the 'guides', which are called **bkahdod**, meaning 'one awaiting orders', and never intentionally the spirits of men and women recently deceased. For most, only cast-off spirits within the Bardo will respond, being those of evil karma and demonic deeds, and will pass themselves off as spirits of the recently deceased. For these reasons, the lama maintains that spirit communication should only be conducted by masters of the transcendental, and never indiscriminately by the guruless multitude."

In the introduction to this book, Delight's counsel on the matter of spirit communication was given, expressing that only one type of spirit communication has real value both to the disembodied soul and to those who are still embodied, which is that known as "spiritual rapport". Such communication seeks no phenomena or manifestations, but is a continuation of personal rapport between souls (both in-body and out-of-body) on both sides of the Veil. It is a communion maintained as a sympathetic connection with those near and dear by ties of love or friendship in both realms, and has a highly spiritual nature entirely devoid of nearness in terms of physical space.

Remember, the soul on the higher astral plane dwells in the idealistic conditions of its new Existence and is not generally concerned with the affairs of the world it has left behind. To call it back into a manifest form through the sympathetic bonds of love existing is a deplorable thing and can even be detrimental to the disembodied soul by reason of withdrawing its spiritual attention from the things of the higher plane, turning it back to the things of the material plane, thus retarding its unfoldment and confusing its mind. It is akin to directing the mind of the growing child back to the things of its prenatal condition. To the soul that does not understand the nature and character of mind-world life (and none but the Enlightened souls do so understand) the mixing of things and phenomena of the material and astral planes is most perplexing, confusing and distracting.

The soul should be left to unfold naturally on its new plane and should not be called back to earth to satisfy the living. The result arising from the latter may be likened to pulling up a plant each day to see whether its roots are sprouting.

So heed this counsel and do not seek to disturb the soul in its mind-world realm. True love consists of giving rather than getting. This is eminently true in the matter of communication with the spirits of loved ones on the other side. Truly, it is a higher and nobler thing to send them thoughts of enduring love than to endeavour to drag them back to the lower planes of materiality for the sake of personal satisfaction.

Let true spirit communication be that which is unspoken and comes from the heart of each soul - on each side of the Veil - as a spiritual understanding and rapport that speaks with the silent words of love. Then the experience will be aglow with beauty.

My personal experiences in relation to spirit communication with my beloved wife, Delight, have been of this close bond of spiritual love and rapport.

The forces of love and the inner energies are things of the soul and remain unaffected by the body's decline and eventual passing. As Delight's body lessened in physical health, the strength of the spiritual forces within her Being increased in direct ratio. It was ever-present and still is. Far more than just a memory, it is a thing alive and immortal. It is a distinct spiritual communication that speaks to me and assures me she is her same wonderful SELF, as being in-body or out-of-body makes not one iota of difference to the SELF. The SELF is completely untouched by death and is changeless. **This truth is not just for me, it is likewise for you.**

Since Delight's passing, this "flow of feeling" from her has come to me many times both to comfort me and to give evidence of identification of her continued Existence. This has been a source of great help (from her to me) in the knowledge that her Existence is continuing, and that in due time we will again be united. Further, her "personality presence" is not subject to my whims of emotion. It is no wish-fulfilment mechanism, as there are times when I crave her presence eagerly, yet she is not there at that moment. Her comings and goings in spiritual rapport are of her own choosing, not mine. At the times she elects to come I can sense her strongly, and her presence is a tremendous happiness. That she is there as an existing Being I have not the slightest doubt. The distance between souls on each side can be paper-thin. If you wish to express it in material terms, **passed onward loved ones are just rates of vibration apart.**

The energies which I have been referring to as coming strongly from Delight are today known as "human" energies and are the subject for contemporary scientific study. As such, they provide an excellent transition point for those persons with a studious bent of mind who seek proof of life after death in the physical sciences rather than in the psychological. For their appreciation the matter can be formulated this way; it is only logical to assume that the spirit must live on after the death of the physical body because "spirit" in the sense of "life" is energy. In the Universe nothing can be annihilated, but is only transformed; energy of one kind becomes energy of another kind. Thus when the energy that was of the soul/spirit leaves a particular physical body, it still must exist outside the body, for it is quite impossible for it to disappear and dissolve into nothingness.

From Delight many insights have flashed through to me. One that may have meaning to all who grieve the loss of a loved one:

"Grieve no longer now but realize that death passed me forward along the path a bit sooner than it has you so we do not tread, for the moment, side by side in the physical world, but death in no way has marred our love or even our continuance of adventures together.

"Look upon it in this manner: While we shared those many years on earth, we loved and experienced many happenings; now through death we still love and share happenings, but with you on one side and myself on the other - a change in position truly, but in no way an end of love and adventures together; rather, consider it as a novelty relationship that is only temporary. For ere long when you too go onward, then again our steps will be in stride along the pathway. Once more we will continue our love and experiences together side by side in the same dimension. Then, if it is our wish, we can again venture together back into the physical world. That will be fun. Look upon it all as new, novel and ever filled with fresh excitement. Only boredom is deadly, and boredom is impossible as there is no end to love and the sharing of mutual experiences. How splendid is God's planning."

If I need further subjective/objective evidence of her continued Existence, there is the matter of love. Delight and I were one of those fortunate couples who were more in love after 30 years of marriage than we were at the start. The years increased the love between us in direct ratio to the passage of our time together. Since her passing onwards, that love has continued to grow exactly as it did when she was incarnate in body beside me daily. What more proof of immortality do I need to know?

These experiences of my spirit communication with Delight have brought great solace to me. While these particular experiences are very personal and mine alone, the truth of what they represent is most certainly not exclusive. It belongs to everyone. It is a comfort that I can now share with all who hold in their hearts a beloved who has passed on, even as Delight. Beyond question, that is the purpose of The Book of Delight, of which she is the author and I am but the writer.

In the next chapter of this book, the last chapter, I will share with you some insights relating to Existence that she shared with me from her position of transcendental wisdom. These insights are important to me, and possibly they may be of importance to you. Only you can decide that. Anyway, they are gifts. There is no charge.

CHAPTER 21

INSIGHTS FROM DELIGHT

The insights which light the pages of <u>The Book of Delight</u> came during many months of Delight's flooding my Being. Writing has been a joy. My only effort has been to organize her communion via consciousness for ease of understanding by others who read her book. Her communications have come through with such love.

To me, this love for sharing her insights speaks for itself as proof of Delight's immortality; of the immortality of everyone. It supplies wonderful subjective/objective evidence of each person's deathlessness.

To my sensing, there is definite status to be obtained in the mind-world just as status may be obtained in the physical world. By this I mean the mastering of one's environment to full advantage of purpose and usefulness. Possibly you can understand this meaning best by likening it to the process in the physical world in which a person grows from a child into adulthood and, through intelligence, character and special abilities, is able to make a unique mark for him/herself in some way or other.

We all know this process intimately. On the physical side it takes considerable time as body growth must be effected, but on the mental side it can be accomplished with astonishing rapidity. Delight has proved herself an Enlightened soul. She has great freedom, and her expansion of consciousness in the mind-world has been phenomenal, penetrating through strata upon strata of the higher planes. Her secret she makes no secret.

"The better one learns how to be one with the forces of the physical universe, the better will one be with the forces of the mental universe, as both are divergent poles. In this you recognize awareness, and through awareness, oneness."

Every so often in her communion, certain comments stand out like jewels; captured truths about Existence, transcendental wisdom remarkably presented. A single paragraph applied to each represents expressed concepts of awareness about which volumes could be written. As a recognizable salutation, every specific insight carries this line: **"Oh, wise one, cannot you now see the truth?"** This must be appreciated. First, it implies that the one receiving is wise enough to understand what is given. Second, it presents a negative positivity which is representative of feminine creativity in the universe. I share these with you.

Oh, wise one, cannot you now see the truth? . . .

"Know that as you have learned the art of living, you, in like manner, have learned the art of dying, and have come to appreciate that Existence is perfect and provides nothing less than the fullest of living. Impose not your will upon Nature (Existence) in insisting on desiring this or wishing for that, but rather let yourself flow gently along with Nature and effortlessly partake of her wonders (note the creative feminine in this) which she will bountifully supply to your especial life. The process is so simple as to be missed by many of those who constantly search.

"If you will let your consciousness flow as though it were a log drifting down a stream, the happenings it will find are the treasures of full living, and, this accomplished, then lift your consciousness out of the log which is representative of yourself and envision, as from above the stream, the watching of the log drifting along the stream. In so doing, you will become a witness to the occurrences of Existence while still experiencing all happenings and the wonders of them to the fullest."

Oh, wise one, cannot you now see the truth? . . .

"Learn to accept Reality for what it is and do not struggle against the tide. Know that all which occurs is a process meant for your ultimate happiness."

Oh, wise one, cannot you now see the truth? . . .

"If you would know the meaning of destiny, understand that it is not a map of where you are going to go. Rather, it is where you will go if you flow with Existence without struggle. It is then that the true purpose of life unfolds."

Oh, wise one, cannot you now see the truth? . . .

"Whatever your true wish is can be yours but force not your will upon Nature to grant your request. Rather, expand your wish and let it, pictured as a happenstance, flow gently onto Nature as a matrix forming; it is thus that that which you envision becomes reality; reality formed not of your own will but of the will of Nature, which makes it so."

Oh, wise one, cannot you now see the truth? . . .

"Nature is the expression of God and as such is immediately responsive to the mind of God, even as an arm is responsive to the mind of Man. As God is proportioned within your Being, even so is Nature responsive to yourself."

Oh, wise one, cannot you now see the truth? . . .

"Nature has energy in endless supply and freely presents it to you when called upon. Flowing into yourself transforms it into the personal energy so important to your being, which you in turn can give to others as is your wish - to help, to support, and even to heal, and in the giving you receive the more."

Oh, wise one, cannot you now see the truth? . . .

"Know that you do not only exist in the Universe but are a part of that Universe, even as you are a part of God which is that Universe. Thus, you can create in that Universe, and what you elect to create is your own responsibility."

Oh, wise one, cannot you now see the truth? . . .

"You search for God and seek to find Him here, or you seek to find Him there. Why need you look in the corners of the room when He entirely fills the room? And, likewise, there is a centre to the room."

Oh, wise one, cannot you now see the truth? . . .

"You cannot die for it is quite impossible to kill BEING. Instead you live again and again and again without ending. For you are made as a certain matrix forming, as it were, a Being of which there is none other exactly like yourself in all Existence. There is no choice but for you to exist, for as Existence exists, so do you exist."

Oh, wise one, cannot you now see the truth? . . .

"All is of Universal Consciousness and is of the Eternal Spirit Essence. God is that Essence, and, as infinite consciousness, is the Creator of all that is just as that which is created is likewise of the Eternal Spirit Essence. Thus all that is will be seen as indestructible even as the Creator is indestructible. Consciousness can change but it cannot cease to be - hence immortality, and appreciate that that which is as the texture of dreams becomes reality as it comes into conscious awareness, for Existence is like a dream, and the activity of the mind is like dreaming, but the truth behind Existence is its essentially enduring reality."

Oh, wise one, cannot you now see the truth? . . .

"In the life beyond death, you will be conscious of yourself as the individual that you are, and will know your true SELF as it has ever been. Thus, in full consciousness (recognition) of your Self, go from life unto death and death unto life and in due time unto God. The stream of consciousness is continuous. Only the forgetfulness of being again in a physical body will intermittently fog the memory of who you are until you drop your false identification of the ego, and Illumination disperses the fog."

Oh, wise one, cannot you now see the truth? . . .

"There is no true separation of you from God or God from you, for there is not duality in Existence but only Oneness. Thus oneness and individuality both belong to you, and your return to oneness is the goal which is not a goal for it is already there. You search to find that which is. If you but know it is. When you become aware, you will see in this the completing of the circle of Existence, as you came from God and have returned unto God. As those in the East would say: 'The serpent has swallowed its tail'. From the West comes the echo: 'The circle is complete, and, as a circle, has neither beginning nor ending'."

Finally, this:

Oh, wise one, cannot you now see the truth? . . .

"As you have BEING, you will exist eternally."

And, with just a tinkle of laughter, Delight added this to close her book:

"You have been reading this as a book about death while what you have really been reading is a book about life. Incidentally, are there any sceptics who would care to challenge the truth of what has been told you of these matters?

"Wanta bet!"

EPILOGUE

In closing my writing of this book Delight so generously flowed through to me, I add a few personal comments in this epilogue.

Delight was an extraordinarily highly-evolved Being. To argue with Delight was impossible, as the moment she came an aura of love engulfed you. To me personally she was far more than just a wonderful wife; more than just a beloved. To me she was my twin soul. Possibly I should explain a little about twin souls. Twin souls are those with lives so closely knit they manifest as one, yet each is fully respectful of itself. This was my relationship with Delight; our lives were truly interwoven.

Twin souls are souls that are of simultaneous creation and they function like the two poles of a magnet in eternally drawing together. In other words, they express themselves as a unit, while maintaining a freedom of independent Existence.

Twin souls have both an advantage and a disadvantage. When they are together, theirs is a blissful happiness, but when they are separated there is a loss especially deep. Just how deep this loss can be I can speak of fervently since the death of Delight, truly so profoundly deep as to unlatch the doorway of death to me, and awaken me to an appreciation of the immortality of my Being. How fortunate is this understanding that death is only a temporary status for the fact is that again and again twin souls will inevitably come back together in the course of their evolvement. A happy prospect indeed!

The intuitive appreciation of twin souls has been recognized by persons of sensitivity since time immemorial. John Donne's poem, "A Valediction Forbidding Mourning"[8] was written in the 16th Century.

---

[8]Throughout The Book of Delight I have included a number of pertinent poems from various sources. These have been included not for sentimental reasons but for the truths they convey in relation to the subject matter considered. Every poem I have selected is directly relevant to the matter of life beyond death, and each carries insights derived from the fourth level of consciousness (Cosmic Consciousness). Somehow, when a poet writes, the meaning does not arise from the mind but from the heart; somehow it comes forth with a transcendental radiance from the heart of Existence itself. Thus I have

The following four stanzas of this prose express the concept beautifully:

> "Our twin souls, therefore, which are one,
> Though I must go, endure not yet
> A breach, but an expansion
> Like gold to airy thinness beat.
>
> If they be two, they are two so
> As still twin compasses are two,
> Thy soul the fixed foot, makes not show
> To move, but doth, if th'other do.
>
> And though it in the centre sit,
> Yet when the other far doth roam,
> It leans, and harkens after it,
> And grows erect, as that comes home.
>
> Such wilt thou be to me, who must
> Like th'other foot, obliquely run;
> Thy firmness makes my circle just,
> And makes me end, where I begun."

As Delight is my twin soul, I have entitled this book The Book of Delight, and, as the dedication expresses, present her as the author and I but the scribe. All that is written in this book has helped me in time of grief, and it may well bring a softening of grief to others in presenting an understanding of what death is all about and more. There are even some things in this book which are expressed more than once in varying sensitivity. If it seemed important enough to come into me twice, I have not rejected giving it twice as it may prove equally important that you have it twice, for these are gifts.

So, this book stands as entitled, The Book of Delight, for this is exactly what it is.

Ormond McGill,
Palo Alto, California.

---

included what poems I have in this book.

AN APPENDIX TO "THE BOOK OF DELIGHT"

written from the continuing consciousness of my loving wife Delight McGill (1918-1976) in 1994, eighteen years following her making the transition. "Eighteen years," she comments, "a snap of the fingers in eternity. But perhaps some of the things I can tell you here will help clarify a little some of the things I told you before. Shall we title this Appendix FREE OF CLOUDS?"

Introduction to the Appendix

Eighteen years have passed since Delight left the physical world (in her last lifetime) and entered the world of spirit. In that time I have never once felt she has wanted to return to the confinement of <u>form</u> but that she has preferred the freedom of the <u>formless</u>. I have asked her about this. She comments:

"A returning to physical form is largely a matter of choice for the individual. The physical world has much to offer in the way of learning. It is a school, but there is no need to go to school forever. However, when you are not ready to step out into higher realms, you will seek to return to body, but when you rise beyond that need you will prefer to remain on the higher planes of existence and offer aid to those still on lower planes yet learning."

Thus it has so often been with Delight, her consciousness floods into me to advance my wisdom. Sometimes she is there and sometimes she is not. A free spirit is not responsible for demands. A free spirit gives when the time is right to give, and what comes through is always a gift.

When she has been close, I have asked her to present for the benefit of those in form how to develop the enlightenment of <u>knowing</u> what it is all about. Her reply has been: "If you would really know, you must move upward in consciousness from self consciousness to cosmic consciousness, as clear understanding can come only when the mind has become FREE OF CLOUDS, as it were." She puts it so beautifully and so simply for easy comprehension, in which clouds in the mind symbolize thoughts passing across the clear sky of consciousness. Thoughts are conjurations of the mind - ideas, beliefs, whatever, and, like clouds you so well know in the physical world, are perpetually changing. Sometimes they are very interesting to watch, but they are not real - they are wraiths - only the clear sky in which the clouds appear is real.

"Please do not misunderstand", counsels the consciousness of Delight, "and feel that there is anything against thoughts: thoughts are natural and are as the mind works, but they simply must be kept in their place for what they are, for clouds taken for reality distort truth. So just come to witness your thoughts but don't get caught up in your thoughts in the false belief that you know it all, for the truth is that you will never know it all - that is the fun of living, to ever seek to learn more and more what your existence is all about. I will try a little to help you move in that direction, so to begin: learn how to play with your thoughts, enjoy games with your thoughts, but don't take your thoughts too seriously, for remember they are only clouds.

"In this appendix to what I originally gave regarding the wonderful experience you will have in life beyond death (in the book which Ormond has chosen to call THE BOOK OF DELIGHT) now add the insights I give you here, and you will come to know what living in meditation does for you in clearing away the clouds and allowing the clear sky of consciousness to unfold infinitely before you. When the clouds are gone then truth comes in: the knowing - fresh, original, authentic, COSMIC!

"If you can understand that which I tell you here in this introduction to this appendix to my book, then what I give you further will have great meaning. If you do not understand then it were better you stop right here. For on the earth plane, remember you are in school, and the student must first learn arithmetic before advancing to higher mathematics.

"Okay? If you are ready to go on GET READY, SET, GO ..."

THE WAY OF MEDITATION

From Delight this:

"Let's start on meditation, as it opens one up to existence. First it is well to understand that meditation is not something you do at certain times with your body shaped up like a pretzel. Meditation is the way you live life - every moment that you are. Meditation provides a pathway to realizing the 'realities' of existence. Someone who lives his life in meditation is existential rather than theoretical. Such a one is a non-mystical mystic.

"A non-mystical mystic is one who is a synthesis of both the scientist and the poet. A mystic tries to find truth, explain truth, and even rise above truth and, if what he (or she) finds in life is not as he feels it should be, he simply rejects it and sometimes even says that it is not, even if it is. My goodness, what a lot of life is missed that way!

"A non-mystical mystic does not have preconceived ideas about HOW life should be but is happy to experience life just as it is, in its pure and natural state. A mystic feels he has a special mission to perform and that something grand and glorious will occur if he lives for that purpose. My, is that person full of clouds! A non-mystical mystic, on the other hand, feels that life is just a continual process of adventures that he is experiencing which lead to learning, and that what is grand and glorious is that he has the consciousness to experience what he experiences. His entirety of existence is NOW, which is another way of saying that he lives in eternity. The universe operates eternally, and eternity is simply perpetual NOW. When you become centred in perpetual NOW you become enlightened - it is then that 'knowing' enters, it is then that truth enters, it is then that you advance from self consciousness to COSMIC CONSCIOUSNESS.

"Cosmic Consciousness is an awareness of things as they are. It is then that 'knowing' comes in and ever increasing is your joy of living, happiness replaces worry and even your fear of dying disappears.

"That is what living your life in meditation does for you. You enter the silence, and the stress of your body disperses, the clouds of mind roll aside, and you exist under the clear sky of consciousness.

"Now you can <u>listen</u> to the Universe speaking to you. Someone once expressed it enchantingly as LISTENING TO THE MUSIC OF THE SPHERES. I like that.

<u>"In a nutshell, it can be said that meditation is not a state of doing, it is a state of being.</u>

"If I can convey this one truth to you in this very first chapter of this appendix, I have said enough.

"But there is more fun yet to follow."

THE VALUE OF YOUR SELF

This from Delight:

"Didn't someone very special once say: 'God is within you?' How could you ask for more magnificence than that? There is no ego involved in this realization as everyone has the same potential. The only difference lies in how aware you are to this truth. So many are so 'asleep' to this reality and prefer to dream rather to awaken and appreciate the reality which is far more wonderful than any dream. I hope I can arouse you a little.

"So many seek to find God and they travel this pathway and that. They miss finding God for they are looking in the wrong place. All they have to do is glance inside themselves: FOR GOD IS WITHIN YOU. Look inside yourself and all the glory is there.

"You are a very valuable individual so from the very beginning accept this as a basic fact and feel it in your heart, for such is the true nature of your SELF.

"Allow this fact be to there as a seed, and around that fact many things will blossom, and then you will come to recognize fully THE VALUE OF YOURSELF. Just a little more awareness is needed, just a little more consciousness is needed, and this treasure of truth will become your very own.

"Once this truth shines within you all darkness will disappear and you will no longer be a beggar in the world; you will be a king. The whole kingdom (shall we call it 'Kingdom of God'?) is yours just for the taking, but you have to claim it. However you cannot claim it if you believe you are a beggar, that you are ignorant, or that you are a sinner who must be redeemed by some distant god. So do this, <u>clear away the clouds from your mind and recognize that YOU ARE IT</u>.

"So start right now and recognize that you are it. Until you can recognize this basic fact of your own divinity, all your efforts to become enlightened are futile. So start with this insight and don't be concerned that this may take you on some kind of ego trip for, when you come to recognize what you are really, all man-made ego becomes so insignificant as to vanish into space."

YOU AND THE VOID

This from Delight:

"Would you like to have a method of discovering who you are? Okay. For that purpose I will have to introduce you to THE VOID. It's quite a journey, but every journey begins by taking the first step, so begin by asking yourself the question: 'what am I?'

"Did you ever think that you are 95% void in the physical sense? Consider your body for a moment so solid and so strong. It is made of matter, you say, and matter is formed of atoms, atomic forms of matter with a nucleus about which electrons and other minute particles orbit in an ever swirling motion. What is motion? Motion is vibration and vibration is a form of energy. You are vibration. The atoms that form your form are like a miniature solar system, for you are a miniature of the Universe, so tiny yet so vast really, when you come to understand.

"But mostly you are VOID.

"If an atom, of which matter is formed, were enlarged to the size of the point of a sharp pin, the nearest electron swirling around the nucleus would be forty inches from that centre. Mostly it is void, space.

"Space. Space. Space. The entire Universe is also like that. With all its myriad planets, solar systems and galaxies actually it is 95% void, just as you are.

"Void is emptiness but it is infinitely full of energy from which all matter - both organic and inorganic - in infinite variety is formed.

"From formless to form, from form back to formless from which new forms evolve upwards (sometimes fast and sometimes slowly, depending on the development of consciousness) - it is the way of the Universe. It is the way of your SELF.

"Emptiness is your key, for within that emptiness is the energy of creation. Do you want to call it God? Do you want to call it Void? What do you want to call it? And behind it all is a sentience that directs the creation. Appreciate that fact and you will begin to understand this truth. THE CREATOR AND THE CREATION ARE ONE.

"Does that help you a little to understand <u>who</u> you are and/or <u>what</u> you are? "

THE SEVEN TEMPLES

This from Delight:

"In your journey inside yourself to discover who you are/what you are you will find there are SEVEN TEMPLES you will pass through in your search for enlightenment.

"The first temple is physical: your body as you see it in a mirror.

"The second temple is psychosomatic: your ego in a recognition of yourself and the recognition of others of yourself.

"The third temple is psychological: your mind as you use it to produce your thoughts. You are gaining a recognition of your private world within.

"The fourth temple is psycho-spiritual: a dawning recognition that there is something more to yourself than just your body and your thoughts.

"The fifth temple is spiritual. Within this temple you move beyond speculation that you are more than just your body and your thoughts, and you come to know that you are more. A recognition of the God Power begins to glow within you.

"The sixth temple is spiritual-transcendental. The glow within you brightens ever more.

"The seventh temple is pure transcendence. Within this temple enlightenment comes and you know that the Creator and the Creation are ONE, and that you are part of the whole.

"The seventh temple is the ultimate. Within it comes the knowing of your father/son relationship with God. Transcendence is best described as wisdom that comes from beyond: Cosmic Consciousness.

"If you begin to understand the Seven Temples within yourself on your way to enlightenment, you are ready to begin the journey now.

Begin by asking yourself the question: 'who am I?' At first your questioning will pass you through all 'six temples', and answers will come that you are a body, that you are an ego, etc.

"All these answers will come as echoes through the corridors of the six temples of your being, but when you go deep enough inside to reach the seventh temple no answer at all will come. You will discover your self to be absolutely silent. You will sense yourself as existing, but there is not even a whisper as to who you are.

"When this silence occurs a miracle happens, and you will find that you cannot even formulate the question. First questions disappear, then all answers disappear, and suddenly you will know that you are beyond both - that you are transcendental: <u>you will know from your very BEING who you are</u>. You are here experiencing 'life knowledge' of yourself which has arisen in you, as you passed through the·seven temples. You have never previously looked so deep, that is all. You have been running around and around outside yourself for years and years, even for lifetime after lifetime, without even being aware of your real Self - YOU!

"Understand. In the next chapter of my appendix I will give you a very ancient sutra that will help you even more deeply to understand."

THE SUTRA: HOMAGE TO THE PERFECTION OF WISDOM, THE LOVELY, THE HOLY

A sutra is a condensation of wisdom that has flowed out of the Cosmos - from high realms of consciousness to lower realms of consciousness to assist the lower to advance to the higher.

From Delight this:

"Read that again: <u>Homage to the Perfection of Wisdom, the Lovely,the Holy</u>, and see what instinctive meaning it has for you. Then let's go over it together. Let's consider it bit by bit:

"<u>Homage</u> means showing respect to the source from which it comes.

"<u>Perfection of Wisdom</u> means knowing of the highest type, and that which is not knowledge. Knowledge is never original; it is always borrowed from others. Wisdom never comes from others; it grows in itself. Wisdom is that which arises from the innermost depths of your Being and is already there, only one day it is unexpressed while on another day it is expressed. This wisdom is authentic, and it is yours - coming forth from the inner silence which comes when you stop the ceaseless chattering of thoughts and <u>listen</u> to what the Universe has to tell you. Such wisdom comes from a source which is beyond time and space. Time and space are outside of you, while this wisdom comes from within you, at a crossing point within you where time disappears. It is from eternity.

"<u>The Lovely</u>. Why it is called lovely? Because love is the highest force in existence. Do you not recall someone very lovely saying: 'God Is Love?'

"<u>The Holy</u>. Why is it called holy? Because from the moment you partake of the Perfection of Wisdom you become HOLY because you become one with the WHOLE.

"In becoming one with the <u>whole</u> there is no more struggling with existence and all life becomes a victory. Remember existence (God) is not trying to defeat you. Any defeat is self-generated. You are defeated in life because you fight; if you don't want to be defeated then don't fight. Surrender to existence and then you will win. This is the paradox of truth: that those who are ready to give in to existence become the winners.

"As the Chinese sage, Lao Tzu, expressed it: 'Go with the flow'. As I expressed it with the snap of a finger of time some years back: 'Become like a log drifting down the stream, and what you bump into are the treasures of living'.

"In the following chapter, I will give you another sutra you may find useful."

ANOTHER SUTRA JUST FOR YOU

Avalokita, the Bodhisattva, was moving in the deep course of wisdom which has gone beyond. He looked down from on high, he beheld but five heaps and he saw that in their own-being they were empty.

From Delight this:

"As these sutras are frequently eastern in presentation there may be some words used that are not familiar to the West. So that there will be no mix-up in language, I will explain a little as we go along.

"Avalokita is the name for a highly evolved consciousness (Being) - literally one who stands within the 'Seventh Temple', the transcendental - and looks from there. Truth as seen from the other six Temples of Being is bound to be coloured by the physical body, the ego, etc. Only when viewed from the transcendental does truth shine forth with crystal clarity, but don't overlook viewing from the other temples either, for the man of perfection can move through all the temples, in all dimensions and yet remain untouched by them. Such a one of high consciousness can become a mind and explain things to you without ever being the mind. He comes and stands behind the mind, and uses it just as you drive your car, yet you never become the car. Such a one of high consciousness is known in Buddhist scriptures as a 'bodhisattva'. He uses all means to bring understanding, but his ultimate standpoint remains transcendental. Of such nature is a bodhisattva. The sutra goes on to express that this state of beyondness (advancement of consciousness) is not a static thing. It is a perpetual growing. It is a river-like process. The journey begins but never ends. It is an eternal pilgrimage. It is symbolic of eternity.

"He who flows like a river into the world from the beyond is called BODHISATTVA - in this sutra meaning one who has become rich from his own riches which cannot be lost or taken away. All the riches which the world can give you can be lost or taken away. One day death will come and will take everything away, but the riches which are the inner diamonds of one's own being death cannot take away. Death is irrelevant to them. When such riches are yours, then you become bodhisattva - a blessed one and this blessing is yours once it is realized, as it is your intrinsic nature.

"Possibly I should pause a moment and explain a little about the nature of one who becomes a bodhisattva. A bodhisattva is one who has advanced sufficiently to make the transition from form into the formless as he has entered the seventh temple and has nothing more to solve on this plane. Yet he keeps himself in body form and mind form to help others. He has gone beyond but he is keeping himself for a time yet within the six temples out of compassion for others.

"Compassion keeps a bodhisattva within the six temples for a limited time, even possibly a few years, but not for over long, because by and by things start disappearing on their own, for when you are not attached to the body you become dislocated from it. For a while, with effort, you can still use the body but you are no longer settled there and it is the same with the mind: you can use it as occasion demands, but you are no longer flowing in it, so the body/mind mechanism starts gathering rust.

"When a person has entered the seventh temple, for a limit-time he can use the six rungs of the six temples. He can go back and use them, but shortly they start breaking. By and by they start dying. A bodhisattva can be here for only one lifetime at the most, as the cycle of rebirth is broken. Then he has to disappear because the mechanism disappears, and existence for a bodhisattva continues in a higher realm of consciousness."

Delight tells you very well of the nature of bodhisattva. It is easy for her to do so. She knows.

From Delight this:

"Looking from on high (from the seventh temple) he beheld five heaps, and he saw that in their own-being they were empty.

"Here is being told you that until you can look from beyond (from higher consciousness) what you think you are is nothing but an empty heap, an empty shell. You may think you are a man; that is an empty idea, just ego deceiving you. You may think you know much; that is meaningless. Your mechanism has accumulated memories and is deceived by the memories. These are all empty heaps.

"For your understanding, look upon Man as consisting of five elements which are empty. Because of the combination of the five a byproduct called ego arises. That is what your 'I' is, but it is empty. If you go and search for anything substantial in it, you will find it is just an empty heap.

"Now I can give you a deep insight of truth about the nature of so many lives in the world: that life, as such is known, is empty, but that life can be made full too. Finding that phase of fullness to your life is what Attainment, Awakening, Illumination and Enlightenment are all about. When such are found then from the emptiness you have to move towards a fullness, but that fullness is beyond the conception of most, it is so wondrous!

"Emptiness, becoming free of clouds, is the key. Go over these sutras I have given you with love in your heart and try to understand them. Don't dissect them with your mind or you will kill their spirit, as your mind can only be an interference. If you can look at these teachings from beyond the mind, great clarity will open unto you. Then you will have the knowing of truth.

"And remember that truth is beautiful because truth is benediction which says that all that IS in the universe is lovely and holy. There is nothing which can be called profane, as all is sacred because all is suffused with ONE. The man who understands what I have told you here is well en route to enlightenment.

"You may note, girls such as myself, that I speak of these matters as occurring in the masculine gender, as such is conventional. Gender is irrelevant. Indeed, the perfection of wisdom comes as a feminine element, a mother. It is 'yin' not 'yang'. The mother exists everywhere, the mother is the creative womb of all that IS.

"Does that appease your ego a little, radiant ones?"

ON NOTHINGNESS & EGO

This from Delight:

"I have repeatedly told you how ego comes in to cloud the mind. To be FREE OF CLOUDS, first move on to nothingness and from nothingness to dropping the ego. I will tell you how to drop the ego which will free you from the clouds.

"To achieve nothingness you become empty inside: you drop preconceived ideas, opinions and all such stuff so common to the world. When you allow freedom for 'nothingness', when the mind is empty and silent, then truth enters. In 'nothingness' you can know truth because in 'nothingness' intelligence functions fully. 'Nothingness' means you are no-thing. When no-thing confines you, when no-thing contains you, when you are just a free openness, then there is intelligence. 'Nothingness' knows no fear, no stupidity, no idiocy. 'Nothingness' knows no hell and no heaven. When you act out of 'nothingness' it is not a plan, it is not rehearsed. When you act out of 'nothingness' it is spontaneous. A situation arises and you respond to it. <u>Then you live moment to moment: you live in the perpetual here and now.</u>

"For 'nothingness' to be fully realized, ego must be dropped. So first understand that the ego is not a reality; it is just an idea. You don't come with it when you come into the world. It is not part of your Being. The ego is something that is learned in the course of life in the world. I will explain a little how ego develops, and, in <u>knowing,</u> you can better reverse the process and make way for the wonderfulness of 'nothingness'.

"Consider how ego develops in a child. There are seven doors through which ego enters. It is well that you understand this for with such understanding the doors can be closed and you can drop the ego.

"The first contact the child experiences with ego is 'the body self', which is the first door. We are born with a sense of self and we come to feel that there is something which is especially 'me'. Even the way the body functions is especially 'me'. For instance, we always express that 'I am doing this or that', or let's say: 'I am breathing'. The reality is that there is no special you breathing; breathing is just happening. The truth is that 'nothing' means that God is breathing, as God is within you. Understand?

"The second door to the ego is self-identity. The child learns its name, realizes that the reflection in the mirror today is of the same person it saw in the mirror yesterday. The child recognizes that everything around it is changing, but that image remains the same, so ego has this door to enter by.

"The third door is self-esteem. This is concerned with the child's feeling of pride as a result of learning to do a thing on its on. He or she learns to enjoy doing things because it gives a third door for admitting ego.

"The fourth door is self-possession. The child speaks of my house, my father, my mother, my school, etc. 'Mine' becomes his key word. If you take his toy, he is not so much interested in the toy as he is in feeling 'The toy is mine, so you cannot take it'. 'Mine' gives a sense of 'me', and 'me' creates 'I', and 'I' creates ego.

"The fifth door is self-image. This refers to how the child sees himself. Through interaction with parents, his teachers, other children, etc., through praise and punishment, he learns to create a certain image of himself and he is always conscious of how others react to that self-image. Ego develops.

"The sixth door is self as reason. The child learns the ways of reason, logic and argument. He learns that he can solve problems. Reason becomes a great support to his self-created self - to his ego.

"The seventh door is striving, goals, ambition and becoming this or that. Future concerns, dreams and long range objectives appear in this last age of the ego. It is then that he starts thinking of what mark he will make upon the world, what his greatness will be.

"The foregoing are the seven doors through which ego enters into the developing personality of an individual; and, when you recognize this, then these will prove to be the seven doors through which ego has to be sent out again. Slowly from each door you have to look deep into your ego and say 'goodbye' to it. Then arises the 'nothingness' which I have been telling you about."

THE GREAT SPELL

This from Delight:

"Friends are made on both side of THE VEIL. Such a friendship is one that has been formed between the Master Patanjali and Ormond who has been script writer for my presented perceptions. The ol' boy is equally a friend of mine. Patanjali is Hindu and he tells of THE GREAT SPELL which provides an excellent way for me to wind up this appendix to my book and climax what I have given you with my love. So here are these instructions from the East to the West, as Patanjali (oft called 'The Father of Yoga') told such to me:

THEREFORE, THE ONLY THING WORTH KNOWING IS THE PRAJNAPARAMITA AS THE GREAT SPELL, THE SPELL OF GREAT KNOWLEDGE, THE UTMOST SPELL, THE UNEQUALLED SPELL, ALLAYER OF ALL SUFFERING, IN TRUTH - FOR WHAT COULD GO WRONG? BY THE PRAJNAPARAMITA HAS THIS SPELL BEEN DELIVERED. IT RUNS LIKE THIS: GONE, GONE, GONE BEYOND, GONE ALTOGETHER BEYOND. OH, WHAT AN AWAKENING. ALL HAIL! THIS COMPLETES THE HEART OF PERFECT WISDOM.'

"Until you understand what is given here, it means nothing. When you understand, it means everything. I will try to help you understand what Patanjali is saying.

"THE GREAT SPELL is a technique to take away your problems, your illusions, and when the illusions are taken away, that which remains is truth.

"What Patanjali has given you here is really a yogic form of mantra, so appreciate that the mantra can only take the false, it cannot give you the real - however that is enough, for once the false is taken - once the false is understood as false - then truth arises. And truth is liberation. That is why this mantra of THE GREAT SPELL is so powerful, as it is enough to allay all your suffering. Just this mantra alone will do all that is necessary, for in truth <u>what could</u> go wrong, as Patanjali told it to me? Truth to Patanjali means 'it is the case'.

"THE GREAT SPELL starts: <u>Therefore, the only thing worth knowing,</u> which is the conclusion of what I have given you in this appendix. It is presented between two energies: you and me, and you have not said a single word. You have remained silent, because in seeking the way of life that is FREE OF CLOUDS <u>you become a quest not a question.</u> When you read my book, you must be asking with your WHOLE BEING, not just your mind. Otherwise you are wasting your time reading it. When you truly seek to know the truth about your immortality, your very existence turns into a question mark, and your whole being becomes thirsty for such knowing. In every way I hope I have helped satisfy such thirst.

"So these ultimate instructions begin by stating: <u>Therefore,the only thing worth knowing is the prajnaparamita</u> which condenses all the teaching of this Master into one small paragraph. It is the formula for entering what Buddha calls 'Nirvana'; for entering what Christ calls 'The Kingdom of God', what you may call 'Cosmic Consciousness' and/or 'Enlightenment'. So:

<u>Therefore the only thing worth knowing is the prajnaparamita (prajnaparamita in Sanskrit means 'insight into truth') as THE GREAT SPELL, the spell of great knowledge, the utmost spell, the unequalled spell, allayer of all suffering, in truth - for what could go wrong? By the Prajnaparamita has this spell been delivered. It runs like this: Gone, gone, gone beyond, gone altogether beyond. Oh, what an awakening. All hail! This completes the heart of perfect wisdom.'</u>

"As I have mentioned, the formula is given you in mantra form. A mantra helps you to understand. It is a spell, a magic formula. <u>It implies the phenomenon that whatever you have got is really not there, and whatever you have not got is there.</u>

"It is obvious that Patanjali who gave me this formula - this magic spell - held it in the highest esteem, as he praises it over and over. Now understand that a mantra is a spell to take things away which are not really there. For example, a mantra will help you drop your ego. Ego is a ghost, just an illusion, just an idea, just a false identification of yourself. This spell is given to take away things from you which are not really you and to give you things which really are. If it is to give you things which really are, first you must have taken away things which you never had but which you thought you had, viz.: your miseries, your hurts, your griefs, your jealousies, your fears, greeds, attachments - these are all 'ghosts'. A mantra is just a trick; it is a strategy to help you drop your 'ghosts'. Once you have dropped these 'ghosts', then the mantra has to be dropped too; you need not carry the mantra any more once you feel the 'ghosts' have disappeared and this moment will come, and then you will laugh at the whole as mistakes, misunderstandings, etc. In these instructions such is presented: <u>truth is that which we go on missing; we go on missing because we keep clinging to the false. If we drop the false there is no missing at all.</u> Clinging to the false is the root meaning of the word <u>sin</u> too. 'Sin' means to miss. Whenever you cling to the false you commit a sin, because in clinging you miss the truth.

"For example, if you cling to the idea of a certain God and/or conception of God, that is false. If you cling to a certain idea of God, you clutter your mind with clouds and miss the opportunity to really get to know God who dwells within yourself. This mantra will help you clear away all your barriers, and in place of barriers it will give you 'nothingness'. In 'nothingness' truth arises because there is nothing to obstruct. 'Nothingness' means that all false ideas have been dropped, and your mind has been freed of clouds so you dwell beneath the clear sky of consciousness, as I have told you before, and which I cannot repeat enough to you, dear friend. 'Nothingness' means that all false ideas have been dropped. You are just empty, you are just receptive, open - which is the way you have to be for truth to come unto you. That is meditation as it is really meant to be. <u>Then what could/can go wrong!</u>

"Further in the original Sanskrit writing of these instructions, as Patanjali gave them to me, we find these words: "Prajnaparamitayam ukto mantrah", which translated means: <u>By the insight of truth has this spell been delivered.</u> That is to say, <u>in telling you this truth you have been given the ultimate secret for obtaining truth for yourself. There is no more to it, and there is no possibility to improve on it.</u>

This is telling that the major purpose of living your life in meditation is to discover the truth about yourself and your intimate relationship with Existence (The Absolute). This you will come to know of as the great truth when you enter into 'nothingness'. Then nothing else is needed.

"Now this whole message is condensed into a few words: 'Gone, gone, gone beyond, gone altogether beyond. Oh, what an awakening. All Hail!'

"'Gone' is used four times. The four gones apply to going beyond the four realms of consciousness: 1. Unconscious Consciousness (such as is found in a rock). 2. Simple Consciousness (such as is found in a flower advancing into the animal kingdom). 3. Self Consciousness (continuing to advance from the animal kingdom into the realm of Man). 4. Cosmic Consciousness (continuing to advance from Man as homo sapiens into Man as homo superior developing a consciousness related to the Cosmos, in a spontaneous knowing of what IS).

"The first 'gone' means gone from matter, gone from the body, gone from the physical world. The second 'gone' means gone beyond the mind, thoughts, self and ego. The third 'gone' means gone from death, gone from rebirth, gone from what Eastern masters call 'the wheel of life and death'. The fourth 'gone' means gone even beyond the universe and the cosmic. In this you have entered into the Uncreated, the Void, into the Infinite.

"In this message it will be seen that life has moved a full circle. This is the 'omega point' and this is the 'alpha point' as well. Gone, gone, gone beyond, gone altogether beyond. In this the circle is complete, and you have come back home, which is another way of saying you have become conscious of your consciousness. YOU!

"Then Patanjali's instructions conclude by saying: 'Oh, what an awakening. All hail!' And it is added: 'This completes the heart of perfect wisdom.'

"You have come back home to the source of creation. What an awakening is yours in having completed your learning of the perfect wisdom. This awakening is ENLIGHTENMENT. ALL HAIL (Alleluia)! This is the benediction. This is the ecstasy everyone is searching for. Your only difficulty could be that you are an Enlightened One who does not yet know he (or she) is enlightened. That's the dilemma. These instructions help you bridge that gap, help you to become what you are destined to become, help you to fulfil and recognize your true nature: YOUR BEING. Remember however that these instructions are not just to be repeated over and over as a mantra, as has been the case millions and millions of times. Unless the meaning is turned into a meditation (as your way of living life) so that you feel it in your heart as well as in your head, so that it enters you as a recognition of your truth, it means nothing. In other words, what is important is that you understand what is told you here and allow it to realize your SELF to yourself. WHEN CONSCIOUSNESS BECOMES CONSCIOUS OF CONSCIOUSNESS IT IS THEN THAT YOU COME TO KNOW YOUR BEINGNESS AND ARE FREE OF CLOUDS."

THE GREAT SPELL even implies one can rise beyond the fourth level of consciousness. Is that possible? I asked the consciousness of Delight that question.

"Good Heavens, from which level of consciousness do you imagine Patanjali and I communicated to bring you these instructions?" she said with just a tinkling of laughter.